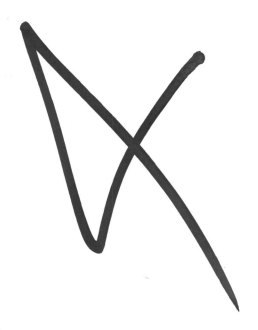

MICHAEL SCHUMACHER

Other titles by Christopher Hilton

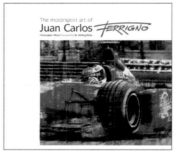

'In order to get the ultimate in performance,
man has always – always – surpassed whatever technology has been provided.'
– Sir Jackie Stewart, discussing Michael Schumacher

MICHAEL SCHUMACHER

THE GREATEST OF ALL?

CHRISTOPHER HILTON

Photography by Rainer Schlegelmilch

Haynes Publishing

© Text, Christopher Hilton 2002
© Photography, Rainer W. Schlegelmilch 2002

First published in April 2002

A catalogue record for this book is available from the
British Library

ISBN 1 85960 873 6

Library of Congress catalog card no. 2001099281

Haynes North America Inc., 861 Lawrence Drive,
Newbury Park, California 91320, USA.

Published by Haynes Publishing, Sparkford,
Yeovil, Somerset BA22 7JJ, UK.
Tel: 01963 442030 Fax 01963 440001
Int. tel: +44 1963 442030 Int. fax: +44 1963 440001
E-mail: sales@haynes-manuals.co.uk
Web site: www.haynes.co.uk

Designed by Simon Larkin, Haynes Publishing
Page layout by Chris Fayers, Morwenstow, Cornwall
Printed and bound in Britain by
J. H. Haynes & Co. Ltd, Sparkford

CONTENTS

INTRODUCTION and ACKNOWLEDGEMENTS

A word about the structure of this book. Michael Schumacher's career has become a monumental thing with, as I write these words going into the 2002 season, every significant Grand Prix record either broken or at his mercy. He must be measured against the very greatest of drivers and you can argue, as some do, that he already is the greatest. The book is a searching out of the context in which that question demands to be asked.

I have covered the 2001 season in detail because that took him to the threshold – and beyond – of the records. I have recreated in detail his début at Spa in 1991, his first victory (also there, a year later) and the race in Spain when he finished second despite being stuck in fifth gear, because they explain how he can do what he does. I've explored his astonishing record in qualifying, and set down, in thumbnail sketches, every victory on his way to beating Alain Prost's total. I've recreated the day when he drove a 1983 Ferrari turbo and, seeing the mechanics in tears of nostalgia, understood that Ferrari was far more than a large and wealthy racing team. And I've posed the big question: is he the greatest of all?

There is an historical feel to the book because it's about Schumacher's place in the life of the World Championship, which began in 1950. He has lifted himself to a level where it is impossible to discuss him in any other terms.

I am particularly thankful to Sir Stirling Moss, Sir Jackie Stewart and Jo Ramirez for giving me long interviews. Jody Scheckter kindly answered three important questions. Jim Endruweit, former Lotus mechanic, provided invaluable background on Jim Clark. Pat Symonds of Benetton made space in his busy schedule to talk at length about Schumacher's first victory.

Paolo Martinelli, the Ferrari engine chief, made the daunting subject of engineering, and Schumacher's relationship with it, simplicity itself. Luca Colajanni, in charge of the team's motorsport press office, provided invaluable background information. Nigel Stepney, a former Lotus mechanic and long-time member of the Ferrari team,

was as candid as he always is. Rory Byrne kindly corrected details about his life for the Curriculum Vitae in Chapter Four, and gave a precise précis of the 2001 season.

Many others helped with foreground and background information, particularly Nigel Roebuck (who allowed me to reproduce a fascinating interview he did with Martin Brundle), Doug Nye, Renaud de Laborderie and Jean-Louis Schlesser. Manuela Borelli of the Ferrari Media Service hunted out material I needed and, bravely, tried to connect their technology with mine. Biranit Goren kindly allowed me to use two extracts from an interview which *The Atlas F1* website did with Jean Todt.

Stéphane Samson, a French journalist (now with *F1 Racing* magazine), described in detail how Schumacher came to understand the emotion of Ferrari and allowed me to quote from the feature article he wrote about that. The article centred on the 1983 Ferrari which Patrick Tambay had driven and Schumacher would now test. Tambay provided a series of intriguing insights about that day.

Derek Warwick was his usual candid self in describing how – enraged and on foot – he chased, and caught, Schumacher at the Nürburgring in the sportscar days. Gary Anderson of Jordan made Schumacher's first test and first Grand Prix live again, and Ian Phillips, the team's Commercial Manager, filled in important details.

Brian Hart helped, as ever, explaining backgrounds and finding contexts.

I'm deeply grateful to David Hayhoe for reading the manuscript and I pay tribute to his *Grand Prix Data Book* (with David Holland/Duke, 1997). It was an invaluable source of reference. I've also leaned on *Autosport*, *Autocourse* (Hazleton Publishing) and the *Marlboro Grand Prix Guide*.

Claire Williams of octagon motorsports dug out a map of Silverstone showing the South Circuit, which was where Schumacher first drove a Formula 1 car, finding himself in a fast and frightening place, not some sculptured mini-track suitable for go-karts. I thank her for her friendly efficiency.

Chapter One

HISTORY LESSONS, 2001

Arace, a championship and history itself were compressed into a few seconds one August afternoon in 2001 and, when it was done, Michael Schumacher found this compression of words to describe it: 'A beautiful weekend'.

In those first few seconds he thrust his Ferrari from pole position to the first corner of the Hungaroring. This was more than taking the lead in the Hungarian Grand Prix, it was the decisive moment of the race and it would bring the World Championship with it. For the next hour and 41 minutes Schumacher circled essentially alone, at his own pace and in his own time. This was a master at the height of his art, smoothing the ferocity of a racing car into a great simplicity, soothing the turbulence of a Grand Prix into a processional thing, and utterly under his control. The French sports daily *L'Equipe* compressed that into a headline across their front page next day: SCHUMI ALONE IN THE WORLD.

He was.

You cannot pretend that the Hungarian Grand Prix was a gripping race in any meaningful sense because Schumacher and Ferrari were now too good to permit anything like that.

They came to the Hungaroring, the thirteenth of the 17 rounds, with Schumacher on 84 points and David Coulthard (McLaren) on 47, a differential so enormous that the championship was no longer gripping in any meaningful sense, either. Schumacher was going to win it somewhere, sometime. Here? Ross Brawn – most shrewd reader of men,

Jean Todt carried the weight and never let it show. Suzuka, 2000, the championship finally won and no emotion left unturned.

machines and moments as Ferrari's Technical Director – surveyed Schumacher and judged him to be in 'great shape'. The championship pressure, Brawn concluded, has been passed from him to the others who have to try and catch him.

Schumacher confirmed how relaxed he felt and insisted saying this 'wasn't a tactic to stop putting too much pressure on myself. It was just like that, not deliberate at all.' He even told Jean Todt, the Ferrari team boss, 'you know, I haven't got a very good feeling, I'm not sure that this is the weekend we'll do it.'

He chanced to meet Alain Prost, now running his own team, the day before the race and Prost told him to win. Prost had held the record number of victories, 51, since 1993 and was 'bored' having to talk endlessly about it. Schumacher, having to talk endlessly about beating it, replied 'I feel exactly the same.' Schumacher had 50. This was really what the Hungaroring was about: not just a World Championship but helping to establish Schumacher's place in history. He had been in Grand Prix racing for a decade and now, in his maturity, all manner of records were tumbling towards him. Records may or may not be an accurate gauge of a driver, although if he has won more races than anybody else, taken more points and put himself within one of equalling the most championships it must tell us something.

It all began in karting and Schumacher returns to it whenever he can. This is 1995.

Jo Ramirez, McLaren's team co-ordinator and a man fiercely proud of the team, points out that 'Alain had, I think, 30 wins when he was with us.' Out of loyalty to what Prost had achieved at McLaren, Ramirez told him 'Michael is very close to breaking your record and we are going to do everything in our power to stop him doing it this year. . . .'

Whatever his feelings about whether the championship would be here or not, Schumacher established a mood by going fastest on the Friday.

Schumacher	1m 16.651s
Barrichello	1m 16.734s
Häkkinen	1m 16.789s
Tenth . . .	
Coulthard	1m 18.182s

In fact, Coulthard 'hit the kerb at an unfortunate angle, damaging the chassis' in the first of the two sessions and couldn't drive in the second.

Schumacher spoke as he does, pragmatically and almost defensively, each word in the verbal procession under control. He conceded that, if you gazed at the times, 'we are looking quite good today but these times count for nothing in the long run. We know we are in a strong position and we should be competitive in terms of our package. We are still working on it to find the perfect solution but we seem to be close to that point. As usual the track was slippy here. If you look at the times of Rubens and Häkkinen it is very close and I expect a similar situation tomorrow.'

Whenever you hear him speak like this, as he habitually does in public, you wonder if there is a real live human being trying to get out or whether he handles these occasions as he drives: the fastest route between two points is a straight line. Somehow you know him well – the speech pattern, the chewed intonation – and somehow his enormous talent lies meticulously concealed behind the verbal shield he erects around it. You feel somehow he has rehearsed the words and perhaps rehearsed his whole adult life.

The talent was on most public display in qualifying on the Saturday because he required only two runs. Moving towards the half hour, Häkkinen had provisional pole with 1m 15.41. Schumacher forced that to 1m 14.41 and it stayed there until, with 20 minutes to go, he forced it to 1m 14.05. This was itself a compression of a lap, to which he brought so much balance and so much speed that, as someone observed, it appeared to defy physics. Coulthard produced a forceful lap to join him on the front row *but 0.801 seconds slower*. In historical terms this is what such a gap really represented set against the preceding five years:

1996 (Schumacher from Hill)	0.05
1997 (Schumacher from Villeneuve)	0.1
1998 (Häkkinen from Coulthard)	0.1
1999 (Häkkinen from Coulthard)	0.1
2000 (Schumacher from Coulthard)	0.3
2001 (Schumacher from Coulthard)	0.8

Horrific moment on the long journey to Budapest, 2001. At Hockenheim Luciano Burti (Prost) couldn't avoid Schumacher's Ferrari, which had a gearbox problem.

Schumacher stayed true to his central philosophy of the pragmatism although he did allow in a superlative or two. Psychology? It certainly can't have helped Coulthard. 'I am surprised at this lap time because it is much quicker than our predictions suggested,' Schumacher said. 'It's the result of a perfect lap and a car that was already 100% in the morning. I only did six laps' – out lap, fast lap, in lap, twice – 'but not to save tyres. I just felt I had got the maximum out of myself and the car so it was better to sit rather than waste effort. Of course I will be trying to win tomorrow but I do not expect the advantage to be as big as today. I do expect a tight, competitive race with Rubens and David. It should be a good show for the spectators.'

Now Brawn said: 'An exceptional performance from Michael. The fact that he won the championship last year has made this season less stressful for him. I have seen no signs of pressure.'

The mood at Budapest. From the grid into the parade lap you lay rubber so you'll have grip when the race begins.

Coulthard, approaching the race, said he'd prefer to finish the season second in the table than third, obviously, but 'it's only another trophy in the cabinet and it doesn't give you WC after your name' – World Champion. Maybe Coulthard smiled at the *double entendre* and maybe he didn't.

The Hungaroring is fashioned out of dips and rises with a vast bank on the left of the grid and there Schumacher's supporters were so many – thousands upon thousands – that it might have been Germany; and they thundered their approval when he brought the Ferrari to the grid. He'd had the car through a gravel trap on the warm-up lap – at Turn 12, the right-hander before the left-loop and the pits – and that stirred a flurry of activity from the mechanics when he'd settled it on the bay for pole.

He led them round on the parade lap, knowing that historically he who reaches Turn 1 in the lead can commandeer and then command the race from there. At the instant the five red lights blinked off Schumacher was away, Barrichello working a path in behind him and going over to the right, masking Turn 1 from Coulthard. Schumacher, ahead, was away free.

And that was the completion of the compression.

Barrichello would ride shotgun behind, masking Coulthard from the whole maddening point-and-squirt circuit. Completing the opening lap Schumacher had siphoned out a lead of 1.3 seconds, next lap it was 1.3, the lap after that 1.3, then 1.2, then 1.4. On lap 7 it was 1.3, and Coulthard was hammering out fastest lap after fastest lap but still Barrichello stayed ahead of him. And on lap 9 Barrichello cut the gap to Schumacher to 0.9 seconds.

The received wisdom – born, nurtured and confirmed during Schumacher's decade of Grand Prix racing – was that if you gave him the lead you didn't see him again, never mind cut gaps. Here at the Hungaroring he was happy to go round and round preserving, as he would say, his tyres 'for later' and when he was satisfied that he was doing that he simply accelerated. The fractions are important to underscore how it happened.

On lap 10 he had restored the gap to 1.3 seconds, on lap 11 he set fastest lap and extended the lead to 2.7 (Coulthard @ 3.4), on lap 12 it was 3.4 – fastest lap again – and out it went, to 4.1, 4.4, 5.3 (fastest lap).

It is true that Barrichello's car was 'a bit difficult on my first set of tyres' but that scarcely affected Schumacher who, on lap 16, set fastest lap again and that broke the record set by Nigel Mansell in 1992. By the posture of the Ferrari on the track you would never have known Schumacher had just done such a thing, because this was the control of a master: to settle himself and the car down and, when he was ready, to increase his pace to the point where nobody else could stay with it while never looking faster. He skimmed smoothly through the corners just as he had done on the slower laps, the car never skipping or stuttering but held forever poised in a beautiful balance. The record seemed almost an incidental by-product of the inevitability.

It is one of those things the very greatest can do, go fast *slowly* whenever they wish, while their fellow drivers run breathless to try and stay with them. The modern car, so sophisticated that finding advantages over the other cars is frustrating and elusive, would seem to prevent this – at least to the degree that Schumacher could do it. The fact that he could and had, here and everywhere else, for nearly the whole of his decade, argued that his career would now have to be

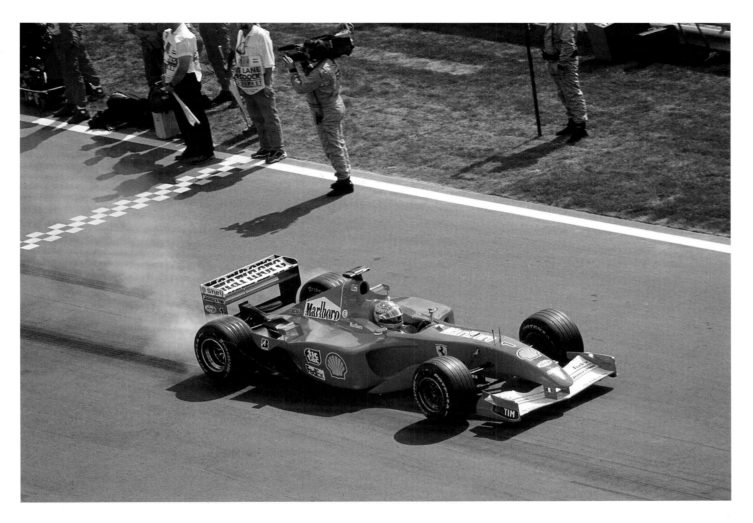

judged against the other great ones. We shall be doing that.

The rest passed into history itself, Schumacher pitting and regaining the lead, repeating this at the second pit stops then cantering it. He'd say that 'later in the race' Barrichello 'gave me a lot of pressure.' It was a polite and sincere thing to say. He'd add that 'towards the end I was worried about making a mistake because one car was leaving oil on the track.' He needn't have worried. He did not permit himself to think he would take the championship until three laps from the end when he thought 'now this has the feeling of it being here, truly!' He won it by some four seconds and on

the slowing down lap couldn't find the words to radio to the team so he said it was 'amazing. It is so lovely to work with you guys.'

Coulthard finished third.

'I might be a good driver but I am not good at finding the right words to describe this,' Schumacher would say. He paid due tribute to the team. 'They are wonderful guys and we have stuck together through the good and the bad times and I am really in love with all of them.'

This was his fourth championship, drawing level with Prost, so that only Juan-Manuel Fangio's five remained to beat. Out of interest, this is the group on three championships which Schumacher had now left: Sir Jack Brabham, Sir Jackie Stewart, Niki Lauda, Nelson Piquet and Ayrton Senna.

Only one man had ever won back-to-back championships with Ferrari: Alberto Ascari in 1952–53. Several factors had helped him, apart from the fact that he was a superb driver. The Ferrari proved to be the dominant car in both seasons and Fangio was absent in 1952. Ascari, moreover, was competing against small fields and many of the drivers were known for competence rather than conquest. Arguably, Schumacher had had it tougher against Häkkinen and Coulthard at McLaren, and brother Ralf and Juan-Pablo Montoya at resurgent Williams.

Moving into the 2001 season Schumacher was celebrating a decade of Grand Prix racing and by now records were coming steadily into view. This was the natural consequence of sustained success. You can have ambivalent feelings about the relevance of records themselves, and how accurate they are as a gauge, but when many of the major *all-time* records are at a man's mercy you cannot ignore them. Beginning 2001, this was the situation.

Budapest. An amphitheatre, hypnotised.

Prost had most points (798.5), Schumacher next (678). With 17 races in 2001, Prost's total was potentially vulnerable.

Senna had most poles (65), Clark and Prost 33, Schumacher and Nigel Mansell 32. Senna's total would be completely out of reach for at least three seasons.

Prost had most wins (51), Schumacher 44, Senna 41. Prost's total was very vulnerable.

Prost and Schumacher shared the number of fastest laps (41) from Mansell, 30. That would go very quickly, probably at the first race.

Curious. So much in Grand Prix racing happens without publicity or fuss, in exact contrast to the very public racing and record-breaking. Ferrari's 2001 season actually began on 15 January at Jerez where Luca Badoer, their test driver, worked on set-ups and tyres in the 2000 car. Schumacher moved into the season on 23 January at Barcelona, also

working on set-ups and tyre testing in the 2000 car. 'I feel well. I had a good rest and I am in top form.' The new car, the F-2001, was launched at the Fiorano circuit on 29 January, Schumacher making all the right noises.

Jacques Villeneuve had made quite other noises at the launch of the new BAR, that same week. Villeneuve and Schumacher had had a sharp relationship for years and now Villeneuve said he had qualms about racing Schumacher because 'you don't know if the track will be wide enough, you don't know if he has seen you and it is very difficult to judge, whereas with Mika [Häkkinen], he thinks like a normal human being.'

It is true that Schumacher often adopted robust tactics at the start of a race, ruthlessly protecting his lead from the lights to the first corner, but apart from that, what Villeneuve implied seemed largely to have disappeared: the crashes with Damon Hill, Villeneuve and even David Coulthard, and the anger they had brought, were years ago. In Formula 1 terms, Schumacher was now into comfortable middle-age and supervising the kids rather than barging and bumping a path through them.

He drove the new car at Fiorano on 1 February, and rather solemnly Ferrari pointed out that it 'carried the Number 1 for the first time'. No Ferrari had done that since 1980, driven by Jody Scheckter, the 1979 World Champion. It was a complete generation away, so complete that the last of that year's drivers to retire – Riccardo Patrese – did so in 1993.

Ferrari reported: 'Schumacher drove the installation lap at 9.40 in the presence of President Luca di Montezemolo, Sporting Director Jean Todt and Technical Directors Ross Brawn and Paolo Martinelli. Testing ended at 17.30 and the car ran throughout without any technical problems. It covered a total of 68 laps, with a best time of 59.505s.'

Schumacher said 'the first impression is very good. The car is very competitive.' He hadn't slept well before the test, 'I was a little bit nervous', but he wasn't nervous after it.

He did not, however, manage a run of a full Grand Prix distance before the first race, at Melbourne, and the first race is invariably an accurate guide to the rest of the season. The fast cars are already fast, the slower cars will have enormous difficulty making up the difference.

Schumacher crashed heavily on the Friday. Under yellow flags 'I was really on the limit. I touched the brakes a little bit harder to slow down enough for the situation and that's why I lost the back end. It was not actually a heavy impact because I did not hit the wall, so it was just a gentle roll and I am fine.' The pictures of this roll looked very spectacular indeed.

Next day he put the F-2001 on pole, from Barrichello, and throughout the race he led except for the pit stops. 'I made a great start as a result of all the practice we did over the winter. Then I tried to split my race into a rhythm, to be fast when I needed to and not overdrive the car. At the end I slowed my pace because the important thing is to win, not the margin you do it by. I just wanted to bring the car home.' Coulthard drew right up and finished only a fraction of a second behind, which meant nothing. Schumacher had now matured to the point where he could pace himself as if the others weren't there, drive comparatively slowly when he wished and *still* win.

Budapest. The amphitheatre moved.

During the race a marshal was killed when a wheel from Villeneuve's car struck him. Schumacher, shocked like everybody else, said 'we must see what can be done to improve their working conditions from a safety point of view.' People convinced that Schumacher was a cold and calculating man had somehow to reconcile this with the way he betrayed the most human emotions – including tears at the death of a marshal at Monza the previous season – and invariably found the right words to cover the sombre moments. This was a long way from the man Villeneuve implied: he'd become a spokesman for safety, and of such personal stature that when he spoke everybody had to listen.

He took pole in Malaysia in direct competition with Ralf (who qualified third) and quipped 'I think our parents' heartbeats must have been high and that they were more nervous than us.' He made a powerful start to the race, Barrichello behind him but on the third lap rain fell and both Ferraris skated off like synchronised swimmers: initially they followed each other across a gravel trap. Schumacher 'could see the barrier coming and I thought it was over.' By the time they'd reached the grassy area on the far side of the gravel Barrichello had 'overtaken' Schumacher. They resumed with Barrichello third, Schumacher seventh and the rain becoming a tempest. Cars were going off everywhere, the race no longer synchronised swimming but ice skating. The Safety Car came out.

The Ferraris pitted on lap 4 but by now the confusion of the race had reached into the team. Brawn saw Barrichello skate off a second time and assumed, incorrectly, that Schumacher was now in front of him again. The mechanics assumed Schumacher would be pitting first and were ready for him – and Barrichello arrived. In this confusion they fitted Schumacher's tyres to Barrichello's car and had to take them off again. Barrichello was stationary for 72 seconds, Schumacher patiently waiting his turn parked behind him. Schumacher's pit stop took 8.0 seconds but, cumulatively, lasted 80 seconds plus the time it had taken him to slow and would now take getting back to the track.

It is at such moments that Schumacher presents his willpower, his breadth of vision and his ability to apply genius to racecraft. Where so many drivers would accept that the race had gone from them, he saw only advantages to be exploited.

He had intermediate tyres on and the circuit was a monsoon on one side, dry on the other. That was one method of exploitation, sailing safely through the monsoon, accelerating into the dry.

The Safety Car circled so that he and Barrichello would catch up the snake of cars following it and, when the re-start came, they would have regained most of the time lost in the pits – something else to be exploited (no matter that, as Schumacher joined the tail of the snake, 'the conditions were atrocious and undrivable, and at times the Safety Car was quicker than us').

No man on earth could stay with Schumacher in a monsoon – something else to be exploited.

At that re-start, on lap 11, Barrichello ran tenth and Schumacher eleventh. Completing that lap Barrichello was up to eighth, Schumacher ninth, @ 10.06 seconds from the leader, Coulthard.

In the rolling spray the sleek-nosed Ferraris were moving

like a pair of sharks. Schumacher overtook Barrichello and they hunted down Jarno Trulli in the Jordan: Schumacher sixth, @ 8.91 from Coulthard. They hunted down Frentzen in the other Jordan, Schumacher describing a great arc of power outside him. Schumacher drew up to Ralf and dealt with him almost immediately. And, describing another great arc, went outside Häkkinen. On lap 13 Schumacher was third, @ 6.27 from Coulthard. He caught Jos Verstappen (Arrows) and pressured him, placed the Ferrari inside as they approached a right-hander, and he was second.

Coulthard was within reach and for once Schumacher disturbed the rhythm he had established in the race by pushing so hard that the Ferrari shivered. The gap to Coulthard was down to 1.96. He tried the arc of power but Coulthard resisted. On the start-finish straight he squeezed up behind Coulthard, came out and went round the outside. The race was decided. He beat Barrichello by 23 seconds.

'It was my decision to fit intermediates. We knew it would be difficult at first but they would be better when the rain eased. After the pit stop I asked if the team had made the right changes to the car, because it was difficult to drive, but it got better as the race went on. I managed to pass Rubens because he lost momentum in Turn 8.' Barrichello was distinctly unhappy about this, to which Schumacher said 'at the end of the day, we're team-mates and we leave each other room. We're equal, so you fight for the position. I don't think that is unreasonable.'

The records were coming now. This was Schumacher's sixth Grand Prix victory in succession, taking him past the five of Brabham (1960), Jim Clark (1965) and Mansell (1992). Ahead lay Ascari with nine (1952–53).

He didn't reach that – second in Brazil to Coulthard – and he retired at Imola with a mechanical problem. That did not prevent him expressing delight that Ralf won. 'This is the first time that two brothers have won Formula 1 Grands Prix.'

He won Spain, although that was inherited because Häkkinen broke down at the end, was second in Austria (to Coulthard) despite a brush with Montoya. 'The fight had been fair until the incident,' Schumacher said. 'Then he tried to take me out at the corner and I had to go onto the grass because I could not turn in. He was not looking where he was going, he was looking where I was going.'

On 22 May, Ferrari announced that Schumacher and Barrichello had extended their contracts, Schumacher to the end of 2004 and Barrichello to the end of 2002.

Monaco? Let Schumacher describe it. 'In some ways it was an easy and straightforward race because I was out in front on my own but at the same time it was quite hard as we still had to do fast lap times. In some ways, the traction control made the race rougher physically as we are going quicker. I love the circuit – it is always a challenge. Today I just had to think about reliability and make sure I didn't make a mistake. I asked Ross Brawn what some other drivers were doing and he told me to concentrate. I had no problem with back-markers and my car was pretty good even if I did not push 100% because in the early stages when Mika was behind me I was trying to look after the car and the tyres.'

This was the seventh race and made the championship Schumacher 52, Coulthard 40. Schumacher now put a strong run together which virtually settled the title, second in Canada to Ralf – who beat him in a straight fight – then winning the European at the Nürburgring after squeezing Ralf very, very hard at the start. The pit lane wall was not far away. 'The start was a kind of key to the race and I had to do anything I could to keep Ralf behind me. I left him room and it was hard, I know that, but it was necessary for me because I knew I was on two stops and I didn't know what Ralf was on.' After the race Ralf was so enraged he did not trust himself to speak.

Schumacher won in France and was second in Britain (to Häkkinen) so that he had 84 points, Coulthard 47. The championship had become when, not if – although not at Hockenheim where he had a gear selection problem from the grid and Luciano Burti (Prost) helplessly ran into the back of him. Since Coulthard didn't finish – a mechanical problem – the points remained the same. Schumacher travelled to the Hungaroring nursing the conviction that the championship wouldn't be settled there. As we have seen, his conviction was misplaced.

On the Friday in rain at Spa he crashed into the rear of

Urgent and
controversial
consultations before
the 2001 Italian
Grand Prix,

Schumacher
pleading for the
drivers to take it
easy through the
first chicane.

Pedro De La Rosa's Jaguar. 'The situation was the usual one when you are running in spray. You have no chance to judge the distance, nor to see the red light of the car in front. All you see is the spray.' He qualified third next day and won a bizarre race when both Williamses ahead of him had problems at the start and re-start. 'I pushed flat out until the second pit stop because I was planning to build enough of a lead to make an extra stop if I needed to. I made one mistake, at Turn 15, when I lost concentration. I was playing with too many buttons on the steering wheel. I ran wide and almost hit the barrier.'

The next two races were pitched into shadows and personal questioning. The terrorist attack on the twin towers in New York was on 11 September, Monza on 16 September. Schumacher felt in no mood to celebrate the World Championship. He questioned aloud the wisdom of going to the United States Grand Prix – Indianapolis was on 30 September – and, just before the race at Monza, tried to persuade the drivers to go in grid order through the first two chicanes after the red lights as a safety precaution. He finished the race fourth and went quietly away. Evidently he had even considered retirement from F1.

They all did go to Indianapolis and he finished second. It scarcely seemed to interest him and mentally he was somewhere else. Subsequently he'd say 'Monza and Indianapolis were difficult'.

That didn't apply to Suzuka in mid-October where he lifted the willpower and racecraft decorated by genius to a new level in qualifying. He made three runs for grid position and *each* of them would have been ample for pole. The Suzuka circuit is a glorious examination of car and driver, and it demands imagination to master it. Schumacher's third run – which he had no need to make and appeared as a gesture of personal satisfaction far removed from the qualifying session itself – became a hypnotic thing. Five minutes remained so he was out just before the rush hour at the end. He danced the Ferrari through Suzuka's 18 curves, corners and chicane, danced it

The Americans did celebrate before the 2001 US Grand Prix at Indianapolis, the first major international sporting event in America after 11 September. The Stars and Stripes flags were not just symbolic but very, very real.

for 3.6 miles, or 5.7 kilometres, and that's a long way. This wasn't rock 'n' roll, wasn't disco, it had the elegance of a ballroom quickstep, each precise movement flowing into the next. He did 1m 32.48, and it was, as someone murmured in awe, the perfect lap.

Montoya was next with 1m 33.18, making the difference seventh-tenths exactly or, putting it inexactly, the distance between the genius and a fast young man. Schumacher said 'we had predicted a lap time much slower than this, so for once it's nice when the prediction is wrong.'

Breathless, the team announced: 'Eleventh pole position of the season for Ferrari and Michael Schumacher, a season record for both the team and driver. This is Michael's 43rd career pole, his sixth at Suzuka. It is the team's 148th pole, the fifth at this event.' In strictly Ferrari terms, the 11 beat the nine that it had stood at: Schumacher in 2000, Lauda in 1974 and again in 1975. The 11 was still short of Mansell (14, 1992, Williams), Senna (13, 1988 and 1989, McLaren), Prost 13 (1993, Williams). It equalled Häkkinen's 11 in 1999 (McLaren).

At the start of the race he moved diagonally across, blocking Montoya – a favoured tactic to impose his will as he took the lead, but somehow brutal in its intent and execution – and guarded the racing line through Turn One. Schumacher shed Montoya immediately and, crossing the line to complete the opening lap, led by 3.63 seconds. He built on that.

'We had the advantage on the first few laps, which came from our tyres' – Ferrari on Bridgestones, Williams on Michelins. Completing lap 2 the gap had become 6.33 over Barrichello, who'd muscled past Montoya at the chicane – Montoya re-took him at Turn One – and by lap four the gap had grown to 8.90. 'I was surprised at the gap I built up, but at that point we were not sure if the Williams were on a one or a two stop strategy.'

Ultimately it didn't matter. Schumacher made his first pit stop on lap 18 with an 11 second advantage and rejoined fourth. That was behind Häkkinen, who was holding him up. Montoya pitted on lap 21 with a 14 second advantage over Schumacher and rejoined fifth. Once the initial pit

stops were completed Schumacher led again from Montoya and it remained like that to the second stops, resumed after the stops. It is true that towards the end, with the gap down to five seconds, Schumacher might superficially have seemed vulnerable to a sustained attack. So he widened the gap to eight seconds with nine laps left. It was ample.

He had now scored more Grand Prix points – 801 – than Prost's 798.5. He had 123 points in the season, beating the record of 108 he held with Nigel Mansell (Schumacher did it in 2000, Mansell in 1992). It was all 'the perfect end to the season.' After the race he looked as he habitually did, fresh, at ease, challenging you to accept that he had just driven through the 18 corners 53 times at an average speed of more than 132mph, or that he had been manipulating the ferocity of a Formula 1 car for one hour 27 minutes.

It seemed, instead, like a Sunday afternoon stroll. Genius can make the extremely complicated look like that.

Rory Byrne designed the car. By nature he is a quiet man and he rarely goes to the races – the depth of his contribution can be lost in the swell which constantly laps round Schumacher. I suspect Byrne doesn't mind this. Like many genuine artists (and a Formula 1 designer is certainly that) he prefers to let what he creates speak for itself. This, however, is his summary of the 2001 season, exquisite in its brevity and simplicity.

'Michael was under real pressure when he came second in the championship in 1997, second in 1998 and then had the crash at Silverstone in 1999. It meant that the pressure went onto 2000. Since then, when that particular pressure came off, he's been driving even better. The 2001 championship wasn't as easy as it might have looked. What helped us was our reliability, which the opposition lacked. They could perhaps match us for speed but not reliability. I think what has happened at Ferrari is important for Formula 1. I was in South Africa recently [at the end of the 2001 season] and the interest and enthusiasm was genuinely unbelievable. That's when you realise.'

Facts of the matter

One way to understand what Schumacher achieved at Ferrari is to set out what every other driver who drove there achieved too. Somehow memory is distorted by emotion so that the very name Ferrari conjures a vista of great drivers beating the world; somehow memory lacks the objectivity to see how difficult these drivers found it and, in many cases, how little they achieved. Consider that, from 1950, in terms of wins only three drivers got into double figures, and in terms of poles only four. Nor does the list below encompass the 38 men who drove for Ferrari and didn't win once. That is slightly misleading because some of the 38 didn't drive much for Ferrari, but it does emphasise the difficulty.

The list throws into starkest relief what Schumacher had done at Ferrari. He won an astonishing 34 of his 92 races compared to, in alphabetical order, Michele Alboreto's three wins from 80 races, Jean Alesi's one win from 80 races, and Gerhard Berger's five wins from 96 races. You can argue that the Ferrari infrastructure was not of the quality in the 1980s and early to mid 1990s that it became under Todt and Brawn, and you can argue that the cars were not of the quality to win races.

Let's examine that. In 1995 Ferrari fielded Berger and Alesi. Berger took one pole position and won no races, Alesi took no poles but won Canada. In 1996 Schumacher came and took four poles, three wins. His team-mate Eddie Irvine had no poles and no wins. It was very simple: Schumacher could take a car which was nowhere near good enough to win a World Championship and find ways to make it win races. The others couldn't. So here is the list of drivers who won a Grand Prix for Ferrari.

Note: the years next to each driver indicate that he raced at least once for Ferrari that season. The hyphen, as in 1984–1988, indicates that he drove for the team continuously during that period.

	Years	Races	Poles	Wins	Championship
Alboreto, M	1984-88	80	2	3	0
Alesi, J	1991-95	80	1	1	0
Andretti, M	1971-72/82	12	1	1	0
Arnoux, R	1983-85	32	4	3	0
Ascari, A	1950-54	27	13	13	2
Baghetti, G	1961-62/66	8	0	1	0
Bandini, L	1962/63-67	35	1	1	0
Barrichello, R	2000-01	34	1	1	0
Berger, G	1987-89/93-95	96	7	5	0
Brooks, T	1959	7	2	2	0
Collins, P	1956-58	20	1	3	0
Fangio, J-M	1956	7	5	3	1
Farina, G	1952-55	20	3	1	0
Gonzalez, F	1951/54-55/57/60	15	3	2	0
Hawthorn, M	1953-54/55/57-58	35	4	3	1
Hill, P	1958-60/61-62	31	6	3	1
Ickx, J	1968/70-73	55	11	6	0
Irvine, E	1996-99	65	0	4	0
Lauda, N	1974-77	57	23	15	2
Mansell, N	1989-90	31	3	3	0
Musso, L	1956-58	15	0	1	0
Pironi, D	1981-82	25	2	2	0
Prost, A	1990-91	30	0	5	0
Regazzoni, C	1970-72/74-76	58	4	4	0
Reutemann, C	1976-78	34	2	5	0
Scarfiotti, L	1963-67	6	0	1	0
Scheckter, J	1979-80	28	1	3	1
Schumacher, M	1996-2001	92	33	34	2
Surtees, J	1963-66	30	5	4	1
Tambay, P	1982-83	21	4	2	0
Taruffi, P	1951-55	13	0	1	0
Trintignant, M	1954-55/57	17	0	1	0
Villeneuve, G	1977-82	66	2	6	0
Von Trips, W	1957-58/59-60/61	25	1	2	0

DECISIVE BATTLES (1): SPA, 1991

Histroy is not an exact science, and that's why recreating some aspects of Michael Schumacher's entry into Grand Prix racing remains tantalising and unresolved.[1] It is no less fascinating for that, and the essential element – a lean, angular young man suddenly announcing himself on the global stage – still carries the force that it did at the time. From those August days a decade and more ago, all else flowed: the wins, the championships, Ferrari, the records.

Quite possibly the whole thing began on some unremembered day in Spain, and a conversation between two men who had villas there: Eddie Jordan and Dave Price. Jordan, of course, owned a Formula 1 team. Price had worked for Mercedes, where Schumacher was competing in the World Sports Car Championship. Jordan had antennae in his mind which, even from afar, constantly felt the currents which young drivers emitted and, depending on the strength of the currents, hired some of them. From that they moved on to populate many successful teams.

Jordan asked what this Schumacher was like and Price replied 'bloody good!'

Schumacher had karted from 1984 to 1987, moved through the junior formula Koenig to German Formula 3 in 1989 and then, in 1990, combined that Formula 3 with the Mercedes team in the World Sports Car Championship. There seems little doubt even then that the ultimate object was Formula 1. Early in 1990, as we shall hear in the next chapter, Adrian Reynard – who was trying to set up a

A slender lad, preparing to change Formula 1 forever.

Formula 1 team – had Schumacher down at his factory.

Now, in mid-1991, Schumacher was still with Mercedes and there were already rumours that he'd be joining the Tyrrell team; but Tyrrell had Honda engines and Aguri Suzuki was expected to replace the retiring Satoru Nakajima, for all the obvious reasons. Tyrrell denied the Schumacher connection.[2]

On 28 July Schumacher made his Formula 3000 début at Sugo, Japan, and finished second (to the American Ross Cheever). The drive was arranged by Jochen Neerpasch of Mercedes and Schumacher said at the time: 'Obviously I want to do Formula 1 next year, but whether I can or not is another question. Mr. Neerpasch has a lot of experience and I think he can help me.' The 3000 drive was a one-off and it didn't particularly impress Jordan, whose antennae reached comfortably to Japan. The factor which had 'turned me on,' Jordan would say, was what Schumacher had done in German Formula 3 and the manner of his doing it.

Schumacher at Le Mans where he raced a Mercedes in the 24-hour sports car race just weeks before he made his 1991 Grand Prix début.

A week after that, the Tyrrell rumours surfaced again, because Tyrrell had the German company Braun as a name sponsor and they, evidently, wanted a German driver. The rumour now was that some late autumn day Tyrrell would test Schumacher, Heinz-Harald Frentzen and Bernd Schneider. In the great, unending motor racing stories of what-might-have-been, there is another chapter.

On Sunday 11 August, Ayrton Senna (McLaren) won the Hungarian Grand Prix. Jordan's two drivers, Andrea de Cesaris and Bertrand Gachot, finished seventh and ninth respectively although, reportedly, the Jordan motorhome was heavy with visitors looking for a 1992 drive – Suzuki, Pierluigi Martini, Michael Andretti and, more improbably,

Keke Rosberg, the former World Champion who had retired in 1986.

On the Tuesday, Gachot appeared at Southwark Crown Court, London, accused of spraying CS gas into the face of a taxi driver. The alleged offence had taken place the previous December. On the Wednesday Gachot was jailed for 18 months.

As it happened, a major Formula 1 test was going on at Monza but Jordan, of course, only had de Cesaris there. Gachot had been so sure he'd be acquitted that he intended to fly down to Monza for the test – it lasted until the Friday. More important, the Belgian Grand Prix at Spa would be on Sunday 25 August, only a week and a half away. (At least one information sheet previewing Spa, with an early deadline, got caught out and had Gachot down among the drivers.)

Jordan Technical Director Gary Anderson remembers 'we were running with de Cesaris, and Gachot was coming down to test. Eddie [who was taking a break in Spain] called on the Tuesday and said "Gachot's court case hasn't quite gone the way we hoped it would. He's being sentenced tomorrow." Eddie called the next morning and said "he's not coming. What are we going to do?" We had this telephone conversation – well, debate – and it ended up with three names: Stefan Johansson, Damon Hill and Michael Schumacher. We weighed one thing and another up. I suggested that Schumacher was the candidate because I thought he knew Spa through sports cars. I'd watched a tape of him winning the International Formula 3 race at Macau the year before and I thought he looked pretty handy. I said "so why don't we give it to the new guy?" Damon Hill was driving for Middlebridge in Formula 3000 and it was pretty hard to warm your heart to Damon.

Poise in qualifying.
This poise made
a deep impression
on all who

witnessed it, and
made them
wonder what the
kid could do.

I don't know why. It always was difficult and in 3000 he wasn't anything exciting. Johansson [who'd been around since 1983] was a known quantity.'

Anderson's personal philosophy led him to recommend hiring Schumacher. 'It was what you should be doing: get rid of the dead wood, get in some new guys.' What is the point, Anderson muses, of hiring people who've had a chance of beating the front runners and not done it? You might as well hire the new guys who, all else aside, just could be able to do it.

Schumacher's manager Willi Weber had been pounding Eddie Jordan in Spain by phone, saying how quick Schumacher was – 'bloody quick!' Naturally Jordan wanted assurance that Schumacher had already driven Spa, most fearsome of the Formula 1 circuits, and Weber said Schumacher had driven it 'I think about 100 times!'[3] Jordan stalled for time but Weber maintained the pounding, ringing every hour.

The start at Spa, Schumacher is already up with Gerhard Berger (McLaren) from the fourth row at La Source hairpin. He wouldn't get much further.

In fact, the Jordan team had cast their net wide. Ian Phillips, the Commercial Manager and a very experienced operator in Grand Prix racing, had 'spent ages talking with Keke Rosberg and Derek Warwick in particular and a little bit to Stefan Johansson about doing the race at Spa.'

Eddie Jordan rang Trevor Foster, the Team Manager, sounding him out. Foster had noted what Schumacher did at Sugo in that Formula 3000 race and knew how difficult it was to do well in Japan. Eddie Jordan, however, was anxious to have Rosberg for reasons of credibility. The Jordan team was in its first season of Formula 1, had only about 30 employees and very little money. Rosberg, a tremendous presence as well as World Champion in 1982, certainly represented credibility. Schumacher, Jordan pointed out, lacked any Formula 1 experience at all.

Yes, Foster said, but Rosberg's 43.

'Is he?' said Jordan. 'I thought he was only about 38!' Jordan's personal preference was Johansson, who could be relied on to do a solid, professional job, but – and years later Jordan would wonder at the passage of time and the change in his circumstances – this August 1991 he thought in terms of survival and Mercedes were backing Schumacher. Mercedes were many things, but not poor.

Whenever Jordan put the phone down, as it must have seemed, it rang again: Weber. . . .

A deal was struck. Weber would pay £80,000 for Schumacher to test the Jordan at Silverstone the following Tuesday, three days before the Belgian Grand Prix meeting began, and after the test Jordan could decide what they wanted. The Monza test finished with de Cesaris fifth quickest overall (1:24.91 against Nigel Mansell in the Williams, 1:22.55).

That weekend Schumacher, partnering Karl Wendlinger, competed in the World Sports Car Championship round at the Nürburgring but the engine failed after ten laps, although in qualifying he had crashed into Derek Warwick's Jaguar.

Warwick remembers the whole episode vividly. 'It was two weeks after the death of my little brother[4] and it was my first race since that. It was obviously a very emotional weekend for me. I was quickest, then Schuey took the pole off me, then I took the pole back off him, then he took the pole off me again. I went back out with new tyres and he had finished his lap: we'd timed it so that we knew he'd finished – but because he was at the Nürburgring he was doing a second lap on his qualifying tyres, basically playing to the crowd. He reached me [Warwick on a slow out-lap] about two thirds of the way round the circuit. I saw him coming, tried to get right out of his way – up on the kerbs. When we got out the other side of the corner, and remember we're doing over 100 miles an hour, he drove straight into the front end of my car taking off the left-hand corner.

'He drove back to the pits. I was, and it's an understatement, absolutely furious. I was on the limiter, I really was. I drove flat out directly into the pits on three wheels, didn't stop at my pit, I stopped at Mercedes. I got out of the car when it was still running to a halt. I can laugh now – but I was taking my helmet off, throwing my helmet down before I even got into the Mercedes pit. As I went in – I didn't know who the driver had been, all I knew was that it had been a Sauber[5] – and there was Jean-Louis Schlesser[6] sat on a toolbox just taking off his crash helmet. As he's taking it off I've cocked my arm and I'm about to hit him because I thought it was him.'

Schlesser said 'what do you want, Derek?'

'You pushed me off.'

Warwick remembers Schlesser replying 'no-no-no, not me, Schumacher!'

As Schlesser points out, 'Mercedes had two cars, I was with Jochen Mass in one and I didn't push anybody off.'

'I turned round,' Warwick says, 'and Schumacher was running out through the back of the garage. I gave chase.'

Schlesser remembers 'Warwick running after him!'

'We went through one transporter back into another and he tried to lock himself into the physio room of one of the Sauber transporters,' Warwick says. 'I forced my way in and it all started getting a little bit ugly. Over one shoulder I've got Schlesser' – and, Warwick says, Schlesser was urging him to explain the facts of life to Schumacher. And, Warwick adds, 'that's his team-mate, remember!'

Schlesser remembers Warwick 'talking very strongly' to Schumacher, saying 'you should not do this.' It was, concludes Schlesser, 'the old story, driver against driver.'

'Then,' says Warwick, 'Mr Nice Guy – Jochen Mass –

calmed it all down. By this time we had photographers and TV crews and Jaguar mechanics and Sauber mechanics all in this little physio room.

'There are two things you must say. One is that I was emotionally charged because of the circumstances. He was young and aggressive. I am Michael Schumacher's biggest fan by a country mile, let me tell you. The biggest thing that let him down, to me, was the fact that he never really apologised although he was forced to by the ADAC[7] next day. He didn't ever really apologise and he must have been aware of my circumstances and the only thing I can say is that I won the race.'

FISA reprimanded him for 'misbehaviour and dangerous practice'.

Hey, I'm a Grand Prix driver now and it's great. . . The change-over: Schumacher joins Benetton for the Italian Grand Prix, the race after Spa, and gets to meet Flavio Briatore, who is running the team.

That Sunday night Phillips 'got a call from Eddie saying "I've done a deal with Michael Schumacher." I had to phone these other blokes, Rosberg and so on, to explain that Schumacher had got the drive and they all said "who?"'

Warwick accepts that there was an irony in the man who had crashed him at the Nürburgring taking the Jordan drive away, 'but that's life. Michael had some sponsorship and he had Mercedes behind him. And, as history proves, Jordan made the right decision. Incidentally, I always remember driving against Schumacher in sports cars – you know, the hour stint you do – but I can't even remember ever driving against Frentzen or Wendlinger or Fritz Kreutzpointner.[8] That guy Schumacher, even in those days, was looking special.'

Weber, Neerpasch and Schumacher travelled to England and visited the Arrows team [at that time named Footwork] at Milton Keynes, then moved on to the Jordan factory at Silverstone some 20 miles away. That was the Tuesday and, as Foster says, 'it was the only chance we had to do a seat fitting – remember we had very limited resources in those days, a very limited number of [Cosworth] engines.' Foster fretted that if Schumacher broke an engine during the test that would be one engine less for Spa. 'We couldn't go to Cosworth and say "well,

here's another £30,000, can we have a fresh engine" because we didn't have it.'

The seat fitting completed, Schumacher came into the workshop and 'sat down on a bench,' Anderson says. 'His English was already pretty good. He wanted to know how he should drive the car, wanted to know what were the good parts of the car and what were the bad parts – because there is no point in exploiting the bad bits rather than try to exploit the good bits. Before he drove the car you knew that he was thinking like that, his mind was saying to him: *there is no point in trying to drive the bad bits*. I saw it again when he joined Ferrari and initially their car wasn't that good, but he won races with the good bits, leaving the bad bits alone.'

On this Tuesday, however, Schumacher – utterly without experience and facing a decisive moment in his life trying to master a vehicle of enormous complexity and power – was asking the Technical Director what was wrong with the Technical Director's own creation.

'But it's the right way to do it,' Anderson insists. 'We've had so many drivers through the years that I've been involved with and, let's say, they come from Williams. They drive the car and they want to make it a Williams – I don't know what a Williams is. You've got what you've got. There is no point spending all your time trying to make it a car it will never be. Michael was just open-minded.'

They went across to the South Circuit at Silverstone – Anderson, Foster, Phillips and three mechanics – where, with Weber watching, Schumacher prepared to drive a Formula 1 car for the first time. Foster remembers that Schumacher was 'very cool, very calm' although he'd been told that the car was his race car which, after the test, would go straight onto the transporter for Spa. The imperative was not to damage it in any way, especially the engine. With a manual gearchange, as Jordan had then, over-revving was perilously easy and if that happened Cosworth would insist – no argument – that the engine came out. In both senses, the literal and financial, Jordan could not afford this.

Schumacher said 'yeah'.

He went out with Foster's words still ringing in his ears: *this is the race car, this is the race engine, don't . . .*

Anderson re-iterates what Foster has said. 'You could over-rev it very easily because it had a stick gearchange – but with the sports car experience that he had had, that was probably one of the least of his problems. He came from a background where you weren't allowed mistakes like that. In a 24-hour sports car race or a 6-hour sports car race, you can't do things like that. As far as car respect was concerned, he had that already, had it as good as anybody.'

The vivid-green Jordan moved onto the South Circuit. 'You *knew* immediately,' Anderson says. 'The car control, the finesse, was just . . . he was the master, no problem.'

That does not alter the fact that on his opening lap, as Schumacher approached where the little group were standing, they all thought *bloody hell, that's quick* and retreated.

'We stepped back,' Anderson says, ' because all we had was just a bit of barrier, and the track was bloody quick there, probably 150, 160 miles an hour before you braked for the chicane – and first time round, approaching us, he was going a bit quick, and with him being new you thought *oooops*. Having said that, and taking nothing away from him, the 1991 car was a good car to drive, not for being fastest but for being good to the driver.'

Phillips describes the South Circuit as 'very frightening. You stood against a bit of Armco barrier and the ordinary blokes would brake before they got to the kink leading to the chicane. Michael came past us still flat out. . . .'

'He was one of these guys who thinks of everything that's going on,' Anderson says. 'His approach is about driving the car and understanding what he's doing. It's very easy to over-drive a car. If the car is two-tenths off the pace you can make it half a second off the pace because you are over-driving it. But if you take the best out of it, you'll only be the two tenths off. The sports car was good experience for him in terms of pure speed and miles: you do mile after mile after mile. And you have to drive a sports car when it's not right – a sports car is never right![9] You've either got confidence in your ability or you don't have. And it's better to drive a car on the limit, and accept you are able to do that, rather than wait all the time to try and go quick. You're not going to feel confident doing that, are you?'

Foster watched as Schumacher had the brakes glowing in the chicane. Foster watched as he flicked the Jordan through. Foster turned to Weber and said they'd got to bring Schumacher in and 'slow him down by getting him out of the car!'

'After three laps,' Phillips says, 'Trevor turned round to Weber and said "I'm going to call him in, he's going too quick" and then he said to me "go and phone Eddie and tell him we've found a star." So I went off to do that.'

Schumacher seemed not to understand this fuss. As Anderson says, 'well, he wouldn't. He had that confidence, he knew what he was doing. He wasn't a new boy, it was just a new problem. He went out for a run and we brought him in because he *was* going too quick. That first lap we stepped back, second lap he went a little bit wide, third lap I think we brought him in.'

Schumacher found these first three laps 'quite impressive' in the sense of the impression they made on him, but thereafter the experience softened into normality. He could do it.

They reminded him it was the race car, and it was all they had.

'Fine,' he said.

They got Weber to remind him. Weber did and reported that Schumacher didn't understand the problem because there wasn't one.

'In total we did about ten laps and for sure I was forming the impression that he was something special,' Anderson says. 'He did another four or five laps, I must admit a little bit easier but not *intensively* easier because, I think, he wanted to learn a little bit more about gear changes and have the time to think about it all.' Mind you, on one of those he got down to a lap of 54.8 seconds, and that was only 0.4 of a second slower than Jordan's record round the South Circuit.[10]

'By the time I'd phoned Eddie,' Phillips says, 'Michael had been out again and Trevor was calling him in yet again to slow him down!'

The test completed, and with Foster making triumphal noises down the phone to Eddie Jordan in Spain, a price was agreed for Schumacher to drive in the Belgian Grand Prix. It was £150,000. Then Schumacher and Weber returned to Germany.

They arrived at Spa on the Thursday, Schumacher driving them there in his Mercedes 230 Coupé with, in the boot, a fold-up bicycle, and thereby hangs a tale. Despite what Weber told Jordan, Schumacher had never raced at Spa before and had no first-hand knowledge of the imperious and daunting circuit at all. If necessary, he would learn it by riding round on the bike.

In 1985, and driving for Lotus, Ayrton Senna had arrived at Spa a day early because he had never raced there: he entered Grand Prix racing the year before, when the race was at Zolder. Now, alone, he walked and jogged the circuit looking, calculating, remembering. I mention this because one theme of this book is an examination of greatness, and that inevitably involves a comparison between Senna and Schumacher. That both thought ahead when they confronted Spa, and in almost exactly the same way, is very interesting.

Weber and Schumacher had discussed Weber's ploy of claiming he'd driven it hundreds of times and, in view of the fact that he'd never even seen the place before, Weber would have to confess all. Weber said it was all a mix up and he really meant Zolder! [Schumacher had driven Zolder three times in 1988 in Formula Koenig.]

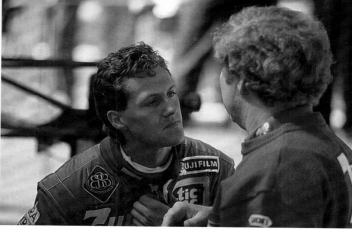

'You bastard!' quoth Jordan, smartly followed by wondering what to do.

Nothing, Weber said. Weber was very, very right.

De Cesaris had promised to give Schumacher a run round the circuit in a road car to point out braking points and so on but he was locked in discussion with Eddie Jordan about a contract for the following season, and that dragged on to the point where Foster had to tell Schumacher sorry, it wouldn't be happening. Schumacher said it wasn't a problem, he had the bike expressly for this, and set off on it. What impressed Foster was that Schumacher didn't ask to borrow a bicycle, didn't ask for a scooter, didn't even ask for a hire car. He'd thought ahead, asked himself what he was likely to need, and stowed the bike in the Mercedes' boot. (To be fair to de Cesaris, he did at least talk Schumacher round a lap, explaining which gears you needed for which corners.)

That evening Weber and Schumacher discovered no hotel had been booked for them but found a room in a youth hostel with two small beds and a toilet between them.

Spa is daunting – the downhill-uphill *Eau Rouge* is regarded within Formula 1 as a yardstick for both men and machines. Mostly the question is whether the driver has the bravery to take *Eau Rouge* flat out.

How did Gary Anderson, who now had a driver with a mere ten laps experience of a Grand Prix car and no experience of Spa, approach all this? 'We hoped at that stage he would just go along at the back of Andrea but he led Andrea from the minute he got in the car. He was in control of what he wanted to do and how he wanted to do it. Andrea wasn't happy with it, he was not a happy camper at all. I am saying that Michael has natural talent and he was able to apply that natural talent without making mistakes because of the sports car experience.

'I didn't have any qualms because you have to give people self respect. It's like standing at the top of a ski slope and saying to the young racer "watch you don't fall over." You don't do that. So at Spa you give a Schumacher or whoever the self respect that they know the levels they can operate at, and if they don't they are never going to make it anyway. You say "welcome to Formula 1."'

Anderson introduces an intriguing point that turns the external perception of racing upside down. 'Your safety cushion gets bigger the faster you go. In a 60kph corner you might try and spin the wheels and slide and stuff, in a 280kph corner you think about it and you respect it. The Bus Stop at Spa – that's where Michael made a mistake that weekend, but not *Eau Rouge*. There are places where you think "I'll have a go, maybe make up a bit of time" but *Eau Rouge* can bite you. The Bus Stop won't.'

Next morning Schumacher ventured onto Spa in the racing car in the untimed session (which would last from 10.0 to 11.30), completed a slow lap moving towards the pace, did 2:12.382 and pitted. Foster asked him how the car was and Schumacher explained where he had understeer and where he had oversteer. Foster earnestly inquired if he was driving over the limit and Schumacher replied affably that he was on it but not over it. On his second run he went quicker and quicker.

> Lap 4 2:04.074
> Lap 5 2:00.930
> Lap 6 1:59.885
> Lap 7 2:00.930
> Lap 8 1:59.254

Then he pitted again.

De Cesaris, who'd been driving Spa in a Grand Prix car

since 1983, had done a 1:57.965 by his sixth lap. Schumacher made three more runs, the last of them – the eighteenth – a 1:55.322. De Cesaris finished on 1:54.794. Berger (McLaren) was quickest with a 1:50.343, de Cesaris eighth, Schumacher eleventh. On one of these runs he encountered Alain Prost in the Ferrari.

'It was coming in to the Bus Stop,' Ian Phillips says, 'and there was an incident between Michael and Prost. I think Michael forced Prost to take the escape road and sure enough he got summoned to see the Stewards. I went with him' – this was after the untimed session but before first qualifying began at 1.0 – 'and John Corsmit [an experienced FISA official] said "young man, what do you think you were doing?" Michael just said "he was in my way – and he wasn't fast enough." Corsmit was wagging his finger as if to say *behave yourself, I don't want to see you in here again.*'

Gary Anderson remembers that *Blanchimont*, the ultra fast curve before the Bus Stop chicane, had 'just been re-surfaced and that created a bump. Andrea came straight to the pits. He'd tried to go flat out through there and couldn't make it. Something was the matter with the car, he said. We spent the whole bloody Friday trying to find something wrong with the back of Andrea's car. Michael was out there driving the car, getting up to speed. Andrea said "you can't get through *Blanchimont* flat – no way, there's a big bump – but it was flat last year."'

Mighty Monza and Schumacher moving to a fifth place finish, getting points in only his second Grand Prix.

When Schumacher came in he told Anderson 'no-no-no-no, it is flat' and this, concludes Anderson, 'was an experienced guy against an inexperienced guy. At one point Michael said "I'd like to try and fix the understeer a little bit," because the car had a good rear end but it did have understeer. We told him that. We worked on it and that made the understeer better but not the rear end. He went out, did a couple of laps and said "you're right." Was I surprised that someone with lack of experience would raise a matter like that? I don't think from the first second he sat in the car that he thought this driving of a Formula 1 car was ahead of him, he was always ahead of the car. He was never playing catch up. You see him in qualifying now and

he's two corners ahead of the car, some of them are two corners behind it!'

In first qualifying, on what was now a hot and sunny day, Schumacher did two exploratory laps. His third run consisted of a lap out of the pits and then the hot one: 1:53.290. De Cesaris did 1:54.186. Schumacher's astonishing performance made him eighth quickest, something not very far away from a genuine sensation. There was more to it than that.

Anderson asked him if he'd been taking *Eau Rouge* flat and he said 'ah, no, I was making sure everything was OK. I'll be flat tomorrow.' Schumacher, Anderson insists, 'had the self-assurance to say he was working it out, and "when I have done that I will take it flat."'

In the de-brief, de Cesaris went on about the bump at *Blanchimont* and how it was no longer possible to take it flat, while Schumacher sat in silence. Foster was curious if he'd had the same problem as de Cesaris and he said, yes he had for the first couple of laps but lifting off disturbed the balance of the car so he'd been left-foot braking.[11] Schumacher had thought this so obvious a thing to do that it was barely worth mentioning. 'Andrea,' Foster says, 'didn't know that at all.'

That evening Schumacher and Weber, according to Adam Cooper [*Autosport*], ate in a pizzaria in Spa, Schumacher unrecognised, while de Cesaris socialised with Riccardo Patrese (Williams) elsewhere. The point is that next morning de Cesaris reported to Anderson that *Blanchimont* was in fact flat. 'It's OK because Patrese says it's OK.' Anderson ruminates that Schumacher didn't need Patrese or anybody else to tell him what was and wasn't OK – already.

In the Saturday morning untimed session, Schumacher did an immediate 1:58.224 and, as Anderson says, 'first time out, downhill flat, never lifted through *Eau Rouge*. He had the confidence not to do it flat out, and the confidence to do it flat out. Andrea took until the last lap of qualifying before he did it. Every time he'd say "I've done it," we'd get the data out and see a little lift. "You didn't." "I did." "You didn't."'

Schumacher was fastest of all for much of the session,

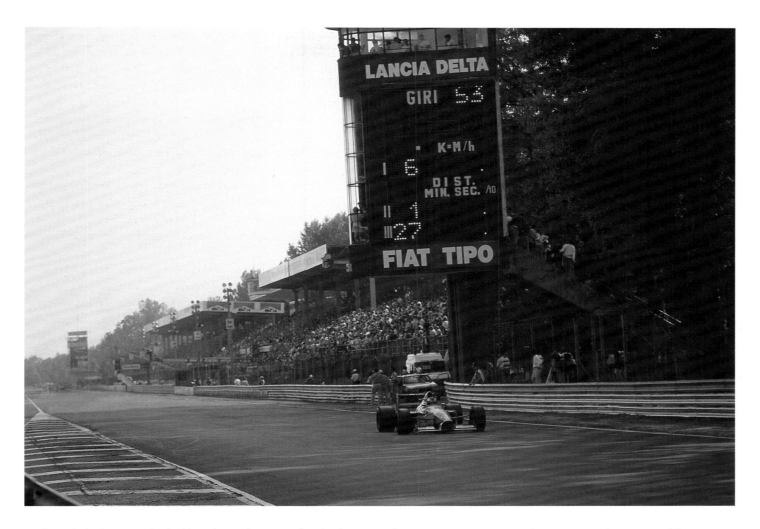

and used the hour and a half to do 26 laps. He finished fifth, and seventh in second qualifying. His 1:51.212 put him on the fourth row of the grid just behind Nelson Piquet (Benetton) on 1:50.540. In the tight corners he held the Jordan beautifully balanced and was flicking it through with the ease he'd shown at the chicane on the South Circuit.

Reflecting years later, Schumacher would say 'when I knew that I would be driving, I thought I would be around the middle of the grid. In qualifying it was better than that, I was seventh, but I didn't deduce big things. It wasn't until the next race, Monza with Benetton, that I was able to achieve the rhythm of certain of the big names of Formula 1, those who represented something for me and who I had thought were inaccessible. There [at Monza] I said to myself "oops, that's happened better than I thought."'

At the time, however, Anderson says 'the biggest thing he was disappointed about was qualifying seventh and not beating Piquet, who was sixth. I am sure at that point the Benetton thing was hanging in the wind or in talks or whatever.[12] To beat Piquet was a big thing for him.'

But Piquet was three times World Champion.

'Oh yeah, but to him Piquet was only a bloke. That was his biggest upset. He said to me after qualifying "I wanted to be ahead of Piquet."' Piquet, of course, was in the Benetton and if Anderson is correct, beating him would powerfully reinforce any attempt by Schumacher to get into the team himself.

Is that not an extraordinary wish for a young man at his first Grand Prix meeting?

'Obviously you said to him "look, you haven't done too badly," but he said "oh, no, no, no." On his last lap I think he had traffic and if he hadn't he'd have been third or fourth on the grid.'

Schumacher gets a corner wrong on the Thursday before the 1991 Spanish Grand Prix as the drivers explore the new track at Barcelona. . . . Australia that year was chaotic. Schumacher crashed on the Friday (pictured) in the dry and again in the race in the wet.

The Sunday morning warm-up seemed to confirm that because, with the car in race trim, he did a couple of exploratory laps and then settled to a long run working down to 1:56.986 and covering another couple of laps slightly slower before he was satisfied. This increased the general astonishment because the session finished:

Patrese	1:55.211
Mansell	1:55.392
Senna	1:56.752
Schumacher	1:56.986
De Cesaris	1:57.055
Piquet (9th)	1:57.612

When the Grand Prix began he thrust the Jordan to mid-track and was immediately fifth. He dug smoke from his tyres braking into *La Source* hairpin and, in the jostle going round it, lost a place. He ran sixth but in the bowels of *Eau Rouge* the clutch broke. Up at the top he found a gap in the Armco and drove the car slowly through, then parked it. 'He was let down in the race by the clutch,' Gary Anderson says. 'A bit of inexperience on his behalf made that happen, a bit of under-finance on our behalf made that happen. He was down a touch afterwards.'

According to Adam Cooper, Weber and Schumacher set off to their youth hostel to pick up Weber's luggage but, returning to the circuit to get Schumacher's from the Jordan truck, found the roads were all one-way to help get the traffic away from the circuit. They made it, as Cooper says, by doing some cross-country motoring. They didn't mind in the least. They must have known everything had changed forever. They were right.

NOTES

[1] I pay my dues to Adam Cooper's excellent reconstruction of the weekend (*Autosport*, 30 August 2001).

[2] In fact both drives became vacant, and went to de Cesaris and Olivier Grouillard.

[3] Cooper in *Autosport*.

[4] Paul Warwick had been killed at a Formula 3000 race at Oulton Park on 21 July.

[5] The Mercedes cars were run by Swiss team Sauber but were to all intents and purposes works entries.

[6] In 1991, Sauber ran two cars: Jean-Louis Schlesser and Jochen Mass were in one, Schumacher and Karl Wendlinger in the other.

[7] The ADAC, the German Automobile Club, is the equivalent to Britain's RAC.

[8] Fritz Kreutzpointner was a German driver who had made his sports car début at Le Mans in June 1991.

[9] Anderson is sure that the skill of overcoming problems and continuing at high speed across the broad acres of a sports car race – the Le Mans 24-hour race is exactly that – was what helped Schumacher finish second in the 1994 Spanish Grand Prix despite his Benetton being stuck in fifth gear. See Chapter Four: Facts of the matter. 'In sports cars it's about survival, really,' Anderson concludes. Grand Prix cars are so highly stressed for what is essentially a sprint that any little problem can cripple them; sports cars run to an even pace, are highly robust and can be coaxed and nursed to the finish.

[10] Nigel Stepney of Ferrari says that sometimes when they've told Schumacher over the radio to slow down he ends up going faster because, by slowing, he becomes smoother and that saves time.

[11] Left-foot braking is a rally drivers' technique, enabling the driver to keep full power on – preserving the balance of the car – with his right foot at the same time.

[12] Schumacher was snapped up by Benetton immediately after the Belgian Grand Prix in circumstances which are still, perhaps, unclear and controversial.

Facts of the matter

Schumacher drove in the World Sports Car Championship for Mercedes for two seasons. In 1990 he made his début at Silverstone, or rather ought to have done. In the Saturday untimed session the car broke down out on the circuit, the mechanics worked on it there to get it back and he was excluded for work done 'outside the pits'. He did make his début at Dijon (partnering Mass) and they were second to the other Mercedes (Schlesser, Mauro Baldi). They followed with another second at Nürburgring, and a win in the final round in Mexico City when the Schlesser-Baldi car was disqualified for a fuel infringement.

In 1991, after retirements at Suzuka and Monza, Schumacher and Wendlinger finished second at Silverstone, fifth at Le Mans, retired at the Nürburgring, retired at Magny-Cours (he had joined Benetton in Formula 1 by then) and Mexico, won at Autopolis, Japan, the final race of the season and his final race in sports cars.

Schlesser lists Schumacher's team-mates at Mercedes, points out that he never partnered him and says 'I was always in front of him anyway!'

The common language of the team was English. 'It was much easier because our team was like a melting pot. We had people from Austria, from England, from France, from Italy, everywhere, so the basic language was English – except when Schumacher was talking with his engineer, who was German.

'I think as a driver he is exceptional. The domination of a driver always belongs to the head. For me the best example is Jackie Stewart. His head was driving all his career and he put his driving ability at the disposal of his brains. You can see that in his career, which was so fantastic. Then he decided to stop, and he stopped. Sometimes you have a talented driver and he has only talent and he wins occasionally. But if you always see the same people winning in different events and categories they have something more. I think Schumacher wins races because he is cleverer.

'At Mercedes at this time it was very hard for him to accept the domination of me, for example. [In 1990 Schlesser and Baldi were joint World Champions, in 1991 Schlesser was joint seventh, Schumacher joint ninth.] In fact, because he wanted to be in front, he listened to everything. He would go out with the car and attack straight away. He had something more, for sure. There is no doubt about that. It is the same today with Ferrari. He has no weaknesses.'

Chapter Three

DECISIVE BATTLES (2): SPA, 1992

'**T**he first time I came into contact with Michael was at the end of 1991,' Pat Symonds will say quietly, drifting back to those years when he was Schumacher's race engineer and at the very centre of momentous movement from 1992 to 1995.

'I'd been at Benetton for many years and, at the end of 1990, I left and we tried to start Reynard in Formula 1, which folded in about a year.[1] I came back to Benetton at the end of the season and, of course, Michael had already done a couple of races' – the début with Jordan at Spa, the début with Benetton at Monza the race after.

'My first real contact with him was at a test shortly after Monza although, having said that, I did meet him at Reynard when we were looking around at drivers. Adrian [Reynard] brought him along to the factory – this would have been early in that year. I didn't actually know a great deal about him at the time. He was driving for Mercedes and to be honest I don't think he particularly stood out. There was that gang of them: Michael, Wendlinger, Frentzen. I wouldn't have said that, from his sports car career, he really shone but I also believe that that is a fantastic training ground. It teaches the drivers discipline, teaches them to read the race, teaches them to look after their cars.

'In the Monza testing I immediately realised I was dealing with someone special. An engineer assesses a driver, I guess, two ways. Forget about lap times because that's easy for

The first step towards the world record number of wins, Spa 1992, with Nigel Mansell (back to camera) looking pleased. Riccardo Patrese is behind.

anyone to do. The engineer does it by the verbal feedback – the understanding of the car and the situations – and looking at telemetry. You can tell quite a bit about the driver from that data: throttle control, smoothness and so on. He had all that.

'We move into 1992 and, yes, I did think he was going to win a Grand Prix. At the beginning of that year our car wasn't a great one. In fact it was the 1991 car because Rory [Byrne], myself and various other people had come back to Benetton, and were doing a true '92 car. We had managed to do a little bit of work on the '91 car and it was reasonably competitive but we were looking forward to the true '92 car.'

The season began in South Africa (Schumacher 4th) and already its shape was evident. Nigel Mansell and Riccardo Patrese (Williams) were going to be strong, Ayrton Senna (McLaren) was a lurking presence in a disappointing car, Gerhard Berger in the other McLaren was capable of disturbing the form, Jean Alesi (Ferrari) was capable of anything. Schumacher found himself in against strong, experienced runners and so did Martin Brundle, partnering him at Benetton.

The moods of 1992. . . Pondering strategy before the start of the Belgian Grand Prix? . . . last minute adjustments with Pat Symonds . . . on the way to the win, here round La Source . . .

'I got on very well with him, I liked him a lot and I think we had mutual respect,' Symonds says. 'I think that you have to earn respect. Friendship is a slightly different thing, it's either there or it isn't. We had a friendship right from the start. Michael was quite opinionated for a guy who was new to the business. He wasn't afraid to say what he thought. I think it's a very good sign. We're talking top line, best in the world here. There's no room for people who aren't dedicated and they have to know their own minds.

'Motor racing is a team business and I think it was illustrated quite well. We were at Kyalami. I can't remember whether we were testing or whether it was the first race that year, but anyway we were running round Kyalami and Michael had a problem, essentially with the car oversteering in the quick corners. For various reasons we were in a position where we couldn't really trim this particular problem aerodynamically. We had to tackle it mechanically

and I looked at the problem and I could understand straight away what it was' – a technical difficulty with the rear suspension. Symonds decided the solution was slightly stiffer rear springs. 'Michael didn't agree. He was thinking of it in very simplistic terms, thinking it would oversteer more. I said "no, just trust me" and we did it and it cured the problem instantly. I think that was a bit of a turning point. He said "OK, this guy knows what he's talking about." From that point on, we had the respect.'

The season unfolded like this: Mexico third, Brazil third. The new car was available at Barcelona. Schumacher finished second.

'I felt we were in a position to win with that,' Symonds says. 'I had high hopes for the car although I can't say to you that I thought we were going to win this race or that race. What I did feel was that, maybe with a little bit of luck, we were in with a chance of a win – because we weren't absolute front-runners.'[2]

After Barcelona, it unfolded as San Marino did not finish, suspension; Monaco fourth; Canada second; France accident; Britain fourth; Germany third; Hungary dnf, suspension failure causing a spin. And then they came to Belgium.

Other than the six circuits he saw the year before, virtually all the tracks were new to him. He had driven Hockenheim in junior formulae single-seaters, Mexico and Silverstone in sports cars in 1990. The rest he didn't know.

'He was still learning it but, you know, the really good drivers don't take long to learn a track,' Symonds says. 'I think most of the drivers will learn 95% of what there is to know in ten laps. The very good drivers will probably get to 98, 99% in ten laps. Getting the further one or two per cent maybe takes them a few years, but Michael was there very, very quickly.

'One of the things to remember is you don't get to the very, very top level – and with Michael we're talking about the very top level, not the Premier division but the top of the Premier division – by being good at one thing. I'd also argue that you don't get there unless you're intelligent. Michael is a very bright man, not necessarily in the academic sense – although he's no fool in that – but he does

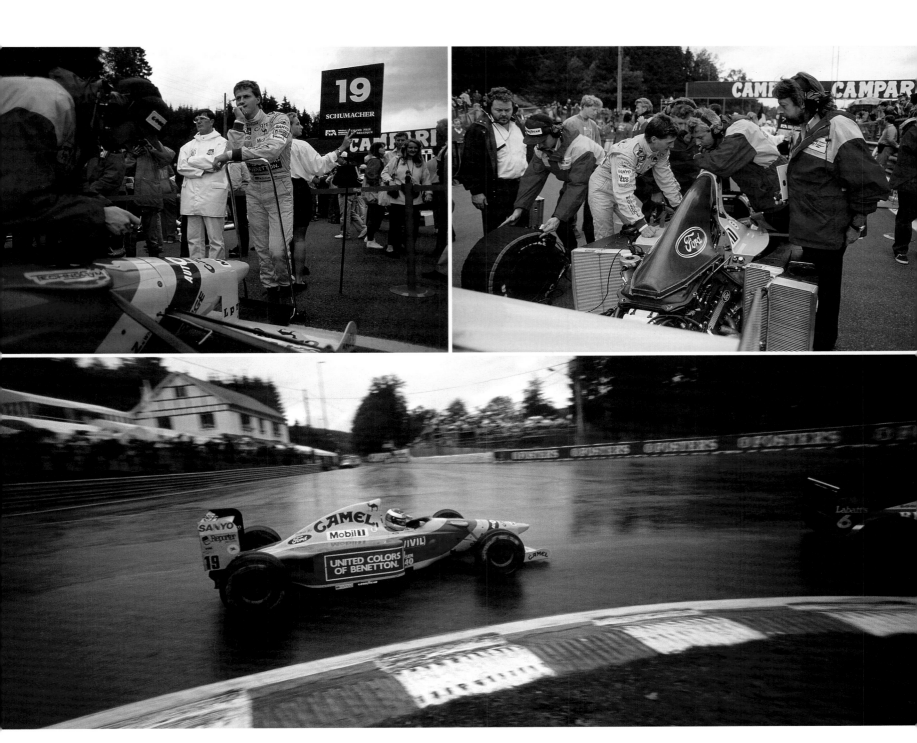

have a high intelligence which manifests itself in so many ways, like the ability to recognise what's important and an attention to detail.

'You have to be in the right place at the right time and that's not always luck, in fact it's very rarely luck, it's normally the intelligence to see what's going on. If Michael had found himself in a Minardi he would make it go quicker than anybody thought it could go and *he'd make sure people saw*. He would do the things that matter. I think his natural intelligence plays a larger part in his career.

'To my mind he was the first driver who really appreciated the value of fitness, and not just appreciated it – because all the drivers train – but applied science to it. For example, when we were testing he took it to another level. The basis probably came from Mercedes and what he learned there. If we were doing a race distance we'd stop half way for tyres or something, and we'd take a blood sample from him. His trainer, a good guy, would analyse that and make sure when he was training he'd get a similar blood analysis. Don't ask me the technicalities, but it ensured that his training was fitted to the aerobic rates of driving a racing car on the pace. *That's* the sort of thing that made him different.'

The moods of 1992 . . . fourth at Monaco, his first Grand Prix there.

Symonds, however, adds an intriguing insight. 'His weak point was when he wasn't flat out. In those early days in 1992, we had a manual gearbox and he was dreadful at over-revving engines on an "out" or "in" lap. When he was driving at racing speed everything was fine, everything was very precise, but he damaged a lot of engines coming in and out because he didn't have that rhythm, or rather his rhythm had been broken.'

This was the young man who arrived at Spa on the Thursday for what would be his eighteenth Grand Prix. Schumacher said he had 'a funny sort of feeling. Just as I did in 1991, I rode my bike to the track. I even stayed at the same place and tried to follow a similar routine – but I had a very different feeling about everything. I had a strong impression it might be one of those weekends. . . .'

On the Friday morning he suffered an engine failure, in the afternoon he spun but still finished third. It rained on the Saturday and in the morning untimed session Schumacher went fastest.

Schumacher	2:13.26
Mansell	2:13.97
Berger	2:14.60

Nobody could improve their Friday times in the afternoon (even these men can't do that in the wet) and so Schumacher had qualified on the second row of the grid. Mind you he was evidently going through the *Blanchimont* curve flat[3] and nobody else was doing that.

	Mansell
Senna	
	Schumacher
Patrese	
	Alesi
Berger	

The Sunday morning warm-up (9.30 to 10.0) is arguably more important than qualifying because the cars run in race trim. In it, the weather cool but sunny, Schumacher was second fastest to Mansell. A glimpse of Schumacher: he strides confidently along the corridor between the transporters, shadows falling in wedges across him, and he smiles for the television cameras – a confident smile – and walks swiftly on. At the track Schumacher found that the Benetton, which had been 'good in qualifying', was now 'for some reason better than ever and that filled me with confidence.'

'After the warm-up,' Symonds says, 'there is a de-brief going through the car – very important, because that's your true and final check-up for the race. After that, we try and let the drivers relax as much as possible (the race is at 2.0). Normally on a Sunday morning they do have a little bit of PR work to do in the Paddock Club and so on, then the relaxation. Then, an hour and a half before the pit lane opens, we always have a pre-race briefing and in that we go through everything to do with the race. We explain the strategy in detail, we explain what the critical parts of the race are. We talk through any problems with the circuit, any

specific points there – these days things like where the white lines are for a pit stop. That's with everyone in attendance, all the engineers and senior technicians, so everyone is absolutely up to speed on *exactly* how we are going to tackle the race. Then the drivers get an hour or so to just sit by themselves and contemplate before they go out.'

In the motorhome, as Schumacher waited after the briefing, the 'feelings just got stronger as the race came nearer and nearer. I don't know why. When I was in the motorhome before the race I had it in my mind that I might have my first victory, and the first by a German driver since Jochen Mass in 1975, but I hardly dared to really think hard about it.'

Dark clouds were gathering over Spa and as 2.0 approached, rain fell.

Schumacher moved from the pits to take his place on the grid. The grid is a crowded place, full of mechanics working as if from memory and people who like to be on television and drivers preparing in whatever way they have found suits them best. At Spa, the grid snakes back into the curve from the Bus Stop.

At such moments you might imagine that Michael Schumacher's composure would be so total as to make him cold, because that's what his facial and body language suggested.

'Funnily enough, no,' Symonds says. 'He wasn't excited, his demeanour was calm but he was, I think, always a bit unsure of things. What I mean by that is when he'd go to the grid, he might do a couple of laps out of the pits. That's not a great time to think too much about the car. With the way Grand Prix racing is, you do a warm-up in the morning early on a relatively cool track and nine times out of ten you're going to be dealing with a hotter track in the afternoon. You have to adjust the car accordingly. You know what needs to be done. You look at the track temperatures and you make your assessments of how you're going to alter the balance of the car for the race. You know a bit more about what tyre degradation's going to be like.

'Those couple of laps from the pits to the grid are not always a terribly good indication of what the car's going to

do. For instance, it's good for checking ride heights but you're not on perfect tyres because you've kept your best tyres for the race, and depending on how practice has gone you may not be on good tyres at all.[4]

'A lot of drivers come up to the grid and say "it wasn't great on those couple of laps but, you know, it'll be all right." Michael wasn't like that. I think we changed settings on Michael's car on the grid more than any other driver I have ever worked with. He'd say "ah, I'm not quite happy, there's a bit too much understeer." I'd say "all right, we'll come down a little bit on the roll bar."'

It made me wonder if a certain amount of kidology was involved, in the sense that Symonds would pretend to make an adjustment.

'No. I would never do that because I would feel that to be dishonest. Occasionally if I felt he was over-reacting I would make a change to the car that I knew was really trivial: much more a psychological change. I'd never say we'd changed something which we hadn't. That would destroy the trust. If I felt – and you know I could read him – that he really did think that there was a problem we would most certainly react to it, and apply the best knowledge I had. But if I felt it was just a little bit of nerves showing, yes, I'd make a change to the car but one which really wasn't going to make much difference, just to calm his nerves down. His demeanour never showed it, he wasn't shouting in the cockpit. It would be: deep thought, then "I think we should do this, and I think we should do that." To my mind, more often than not it was psychological.'

The moods of 1992 . . . crashing with Senna (McLaren) and later Stefano Modena (Jordan) in France.

The rain had eased and all 26 cars would start on dry tyres.

When the green lights went on, Schumacher got lost in the scrambling jostle towards *La Source* hairpin and went round it fifth, two places lost. The immediate order was Senna, Mansell, Patrese, Alesi, Schumacher. In the hustle at *Les Combes*, the right-hander feeding them out into the Ardennes countryside, Schumacher moved inside Alesi and was fourth. As they crossed the line to complete the opening lap, Schumacher had drawn full up to Patrese. The rain was harder, the tyres digging wisps of spray. On the long run to the Bus Stop Mansell went past Senna and at the entrance to the Bus Stop, Patrese did too. Schumacher hovered behind Senna and pressured him – a glimpse of past, present, future – while, behind, Brundle was about to move up to fifth. Immediately Mansell and Alesi pitted for wets.

The driver, of course, is not alone. He can speak on the radio and in Schumacher's case that was to Pat Symonds. 'On the parade lap there is nearly always silence – it would be rare to speak. The first few laps of the race, it's quite rare to be speaking too, because it's a high workload for the driver, lots of traffic around and not much you can tell him. Generally the race conversations begin once the race is starting to develop a little bit.'

The moods of 1992 . . . mum Elisabeth and fiancée Corinna in Hungary. . . . preparing to go out and finish fourth in Britain . . . listening to Flavio Briatore.

Mansell emerged fourteenth, Alesi fifteenth as the other 24 moved through lap 4. And Schumacher pitted for wets. Symonds charts the background. 'I doubt that we spoke until we were talking about that tyre change. It would be unlikely. In those conditions the driver's workload is even higher than normal because of the slippery conditions. A couple of people had stopped the lap before, Mansell and Alesi, and I'd have told him that – I'd certainly have told him Alesi had stopped, and he'd have seen Mansell stopping because it was all quite close at the front.'

Schumacher was now ninth, immediately behind Mansell, and the Benetton felt terrific on the wets. Patrese pitted, passing the lead back to Senna who stayed out on *dries*, calculating that his only chance was to hold on in case the rain stopped. Here was an interesting comparison. Senna, the master of the late 1980s and early 1990s, applied his formidable intellect to the problem of Spa this day and concluded that dries were the best tactic. Schumacher, master of the mid to late 1990s and early 2000s, applied his formidable logic to the same problem and pitted immediately for wets. . . .

Ninth caused no concern at Benetton, of course, because as Symonds points out 'there was a flurry of cars coming in, and in fact even on that lap four cars had come in, then the

next two laps everyone was piling in. Ayrton stayed out a long while – he didn't come in until lap 14. He'd gambled on the weather changing back but dropped from first to seventh from lap 10 to lap 14. Michael worked his way up to third by lap 13 with Mansell and Patrese in front of him.'

It settled like that although on lap 26 the clouds were departing, luring Thierry Boutsen, a Belgian, to pit for dries. That might have been a moment of revelation for all the others because Boutsen in the Ligier was going well on slicks but a lap later lost it at *Blanchimont* and was out.

On lap 30 at *Stavelot*, the horseshoe before *Blanchimont*, Schumacher 'went wide and off. I missed the apex and when I turned in, it was too late and so I turned wide. I was really lucky not to go into the barrier.' Brundle, of course, moved past him and 'as soon as he got by I could see his tyres were blistered and that was my luck because it helped me make my decision to go immediately for new tyres.'

'Michael made a mistake and spun the car or half spun it,' Symonds says. 'He dropped behind Martin and the great thing was he saw Martin's tyres and thought "they're not looking in a very good state" so he came straight in, and that was an extremely good move. One of our rules of engagement is that only the race engineer speaks to the driver so it would have been me who spoke to him. If the driver wants to go from dry to wet tyres that is totally his decision, if he wants to go from wet to dry tyres he has to have an acknowledgement from the pit because we can read a bit more of the race than he can, by watching television and so on.

'In this particular case we were thinking about dry tyres anyway, that was close. He came on the radio and being Michael he didn't just say "I want dries," he explained exactly what had happened. "I have seen Martin's rears, let's go to dries." I really didn't have to think much, because to me that was an excellent reason, although maybe a lap or two laps earlier than I would have done if it had been entirely my decision. I had no qualms at all. We had this mutual respect and if he made that decision it was because he'd not only seen something, he'd analysed it and he'd also communicated it. Therefore it really wasn't a difficult thing.

The moods of Monza, 1992. . . . the drivers versus the Press and if you look closely you'll see the Press smiling. They realise he can really play. Afterwards he had to talk to the Press – about the Press team's performance? Hope not . . .

'He made his final pit stop on lap 30 and from that point on he just charged, once he was on the new tyres he just absolutely charged and this was his ability to read the race and say "now is the time." That would normally be a communication from the pit to him but very often it'd be unnecessary because he'd realise. He's in third place, he's pitted, he knows the others have to come in at some stage and he knows we are now in a very critical part of the race. We would, however, reinforce that on the radio. "OK, this is where it really counts."'

So Schumacher made his second stop on lap 30, and here it was: the ability he would make famous and feared by suddenly increasing his pace and sustaining it to gain enough time to lead when Mansell and Patrese pitted. In the statistics below, Schumacher was on slicks, but the advantage was there to be taken:

	Mansell	Patrese	Schumacher
Lap 31	2:09.01	2:09.91	2:15.10 *out lap*
Lap 32	2:07.19	2:13.33 *pits*	1:59.82
Lap 33	2:11.18 *pits*	2:17.73 *out lap*	1:58.41
Lap 34	2:10.51 *out lap*	2:01.47	2:00.43

Schumacher led by some six seconds.

This ability, which would reach its consummation with Ross Brawn at Ferrari, 'always surprised' Symonds. 'There are two parts to that. Michael was exceptional at remembering what had happened during a lap. That may sound quite trivial but a lot of drivers are absolutely on the limit, they are using all their mental capacity and if you ask them about the lap afterwards, yes, they'll tell you "sure it understeered at that corner" or "sure it oversteered at that corner." Michael could remember every little detail of it down to the level of where a gearshift was maybe not quite as he expected. There was always that little bit of spare mental capacity. He could be running at a hell of a speed – quicker than anyone else – and you'd look at the strategy and think we actually need a little bit more. You only had to ask him for this and it was there. I have not worked with a driver since him who could really do that, and we've had some pretty good drivers.'

Ten laps remained and Symonds says 'that was the only time I was worried. It did look like we were going to win it and in a situation like that you always think it can only go wrong now. It's difficult for me to say whether he was calm or not, but certainly his driving was perfect. He's the sort of bloke who would get emotional afterwards. During those ten laps I don't think we spoke much on the radio. There might have been the occasional "take it easy" from me – reassurance – but not much conversation. He's going to do it anyway. When he crossed the line [36.59 seconds in front of Mansell] he came straight on and he was just screaming' – with joy.

Schumacher would say 'I have to admit I really did cry after the race. I just felt so very happy.'

Then came the curious sense of anti-climax, something Symonds describes as 'the unfortunate thing about European races. At somewhere like Spa you've got to get out, you've got to get to an airport, there's no time for celebrations. The fly-away races[5] are a lot better because at least you can celebrate your win. At Spa, it was a bit like *right, off to the airport*. We are still very disciplined, we must do our de-briefs – that would be in the motorhome and last about 15 minutes, not terribly long. Michael was there, he had to be. That is immediately before we leave the circuit. It's a shame because then you're fighting your way through the traffic and when finally you do get to the airport you suddenly think *Jeez, OK, we won that race!*'

The need to make these unseemly rushes from circuits has long been a mystery to me, although I suspect there are several reasons. Formula 1 people spend enough nights away in any year, the transporters and motorhomes face long journeys home but, more than that, there is a distrust of sentiment, as if looking back and savouring is somehow a weakness. There's a macho pace within Formula 1 so that the personnel – who use American words like 'guy', 'down to the wire' and 'ballpark figure' because they sound tough – must always be seen to be travelling at great speed to somewhere else.

On the evening of 30 August 1992 this is what happened. Spa emptied. The victory was partially lost within that, as they all are, but even so nobody could doubt that Michael Schumacher would win a lot more races and, from these, championships would logically follow.

NOTES

[1] Reynard Racing Cars, a celebrated UK car maker in the junior formulae (and recipient of the Queen's Award for Export Achievement in 1990), intended to compete in Formula 1 in 1992 but never made it.

[2] Any driver's first win is a profound psychological moment, and not at all easy to achieve. For example Rubens Barrichello, partnering Schumacher at Ferrari from 2001, of course, took 124 races before he did it. The psychological aspect is that afterwards the driver knows he can win again – and again.

[3] But he was taking *Blanchimont* flat in 1991 despite the bump – see the previous chapter.

[4] With the limit on the number of tyres a driver can use over a Grand Prix weekend, the actual usage is of profound tactical importance.

[5] Fly-away is Formula 1 speak for the races which are a long-distance from Europe.

Facts of the matter

The great ones announce themselves early, and the three lists are an exploration of that. Here are how many Grands Prix what we'll call The Famous Five needed to secure their first pole position, first win and first World Championship.

	Pole	Win	Champ
Fangio	2 races	2 races	2 seasons
Moss	21 races	21 races	Never
Clark	16 races	17 races	4 seasons
Senna	16 races	16 races	5 seasons
Schumacher	42 races	18 races	4 seasons

In 1950, the first year of the World Championship, Fangio was already a mature man (aged 39) and had been driving at a genuinely competitive level for a decade. He was in no sense a beginner in 1950 and, as a consequence, did not have to serve an apprenticeship with smaller teams. In Alfa Romeo, he had an utterly dominant car. Schumacher's total of 42 races before his first pole (Monaco 1994) seems strange but the key is in the next column, 18 races to the first win. The Benetton generally lacked the edge in the bomb-burst of speed which qualifying requires, but Schumacher could make it win races. Incidentally, at Monaco that year he said: 'It's the first time I've done a qualifying lap where afterwards I was not able to say I could have found a tenth of a second at some corner. I couldn't go any quicker.'

You can make out a strong case for including the next five drivers among the very greatest.

	Pole	Win	Champ
Ascari	9 races	9 races	3 seasons
Stewart	42 races	8 races	5 seasons
Lauda	30 races	31 races	4 seasons
Prost	21 races	19 races	6 seasons
Piquet	24 races	24 races	3 seasons

Ascari was similar to Fangio in that for him, too, the World Championship started in mid-career.

Now let's put in five modern drivers who won the championship only once.

	Pole	Win	Champ
Rosberg	45 races	49 races	5 seasons
Mansell	52 races	72 races	12 seasons
D Hill	10 races	13 races	4 seasons
J Villeneuve	1 race	4 races	2 seasons
Häkkinen	94 races	96 races	8 seasons

Hill and Villeneuve were in the immensely strong Williams car. Hill drove 48 times after leaving Williams, got no further pole positions and a single win. To the end of 2001, Villeneuve had driven 50 times since Williams with no pole positions and no wins.

Well, what do you make of that? Schumacher, faced with actress Brigitte Nielsen, doesn't quite know – although the Monza tifosi would have known. Corinna, peeking from the doorway, thinks she knows too, and finds it all hilarious.

CONQUISTADOR

The championships did logically follow, although on the journey to the first of them – 1994 – Schumacher produced a performance in Barcelona which defied credulity to such an extent that sceptics had to be shown print-outs of the telemetry to believe what they had just seen. And on the way to the second – 1995 – he produced a performance at (inevitably) Spa which demonstrated that a genuinely great driver defeats circumstances, they do not defeat him.

Barcelona was itself a strange, strained weekend. Ayrton Senna and Roland Ratzenberger had been killed at Imola only four weeks before. Karl Wendlinger was seriously injured at Monaco only two weeks before. At Barcelona nine teams refused to take part in the Friday morning untimed session. Instead they were locked in discussions with Max Mosley, President of the FIA, over safety. Out on the circuit a surreal chicane, made of two tyre walls, had been set up to slow the cars.

What Formula 1 needed, absolutely needed, was normality – the normality of those good old days, which seemed much more than a month distant, when the talk would be of racing and racers. Michael Schumacher was going to give it to them.

Schumacher qualified on pole, Hill (Williams) alongside him, and took the lead. Hill pitted on lap 19, Schumacher on lap 21 and he retained the lead. Without warning Schumacher was slowing so markedly that Johnny Herbert (Lotus) flowed past. David Coulthard (Williams) caught Schumacher and flowed past too – unlapping himself.

Schumacher's on-board camera caught his plight because, superimposed on the picture, there was a box showing his revs, another showing his acceleration and a circle with a number inside it. This number showed which of the six gears Schumacher was in. Early in the race the numerals had flicked up and down at each gearchange. Now 5 remained constant.

Monaco 1993. Alain Prost (Williams) is already out of shot in the lead, Schumacher chasing him and Senna chasing Schumacher.

'Spain,' Pat Symonds says with wonderful understatement, 'was an interesting thing. He came on the radio saying that the car was stuck in fifth gear and what should he do? It was a hydraulic failure. We had real-time telemetry so we could see what the problem was and it was obvious we couldn't fix it. There was really no point in coming into the pits and trying to do repairs – if you could have stopped the car for half an hour or an hour we might have been able to! I said to him "well, keep going" – he was leading the race – "keep going and let's see what happens."'

Mika Häkkinen (McLaren), who hadn't pitted yet, caught him, flowed past and now led. Hill caught him just before the tyre chicane and ducked through on the inside.

'He did keep going and I seem to remember that the lap after it happened he lost quite a lot of time [on lap 24 he did a 1:31.503, compared to the 1:25s he'd been doing before the pit stop]. Within two laps or maybe three laps he was not exactly up to his previous pace – because Damon overtook him – but he certainly wasn't far off it. What was

The mood of 1993 . . . braking hard at Imola.

stunning was the way he learnt in those couple of laps how to make the most of the car. He did say that that had a lot to do with his Mercedes driving experience where they had to save fuel quite often so he knew how to keep your speed up and your revs down.'

Schumacher would confirm that. 'My experience in Group C sportscars helped me in this because I learnt a lot of ways of running differently, of changing my driving style, usually to save fuel. I used that same driving style now and it certainly helped me a lot.'

Symonds remains, I suspect, slightly in awe. 'I think I am right in saying when he was stuck in fifth gear his best time was something like the third best lap of the race.'

It was. He'd set what would prove to be the fastest of all (1:25.155) on lap 18, from

Häkkinen	1:25.872
Hill	1:25.874

and, immediately after that, you've have had to place Schumacher's 1:26.171 on lap 40, his seventeenth lap stuck in fifth. Then

Brundle	1:26.233
Lehto	1:26.346

'On the straight Michael did have to back off and that's where most of his lost lap time was,' Symonds says. 'It wasn't actually in the corners.' He could not of course risk maximum revs without sixth gear on that straight. 'The engine was very good, the engine was very tractable and that helped. This was the V8, and it was a good engine.' In those corners Schumacher searched out and found a good line.

He ran second to Hill and, astonishingly, when Hill made his second stop led again, albeit only to his own stop five laps later.

'We even made a pit stop,' Symonds says, 'because we had to stop for fuel and tyres! We discussed for a couple of laps what procedure we'd take, how we'd go about it. You'd have thought getting away from being stationary could be a problem, but we pushed the car to a bit of speed and took some of the jerk out of it.'

The mechanics pushed it with the ferocity that bobsleigh racers use when they are shoving off but, even so, as Schumacher accelerated away the engine seemed to hesitate for an instant. Then, as he moved down the pit lane, it was gurgling nicely again.

'He was able to think about it, think what's the car going to do and be able to make the stop,' Symonds concludes. 'Altogether it was astonishing, although I think a few people realised because they saw he was *feathering*[1] on the straight – but there weren't many that did, and certainly there were an awful lot who didn't believe it afterwards.'

Jonathan Palmer, former driver and now commentating on the BBC, missed nothing, however, although he shared the incredulity. 'Watching Schumacher leave the pits he certainly, as far as I could tell, did not leave in first gear. He gave it a lot of revs and the car lurched a bit as he moved away. I still find it very hard to believe that he's actually stuck in fifth gear.'

Schumacher finished 24 seconds behind Hill and, in the circumstances, said 'for me it's something like a victory'.

'He took things like mechanical problems pretty well,' Symonds says. 'I mean, off hand I can't recall him ever getting really upset about a car failure. We didn't have a lot, because Benetton have always had extremely high reliability,

but he was quite philosophical about it. The car could go wrong in the same way that he could make a mistake. The thing is he's a team player. There are certainly some drivers around who feel that everything revolves around them and if the car breaks they'll scream at the team. What they don't realise is that the whole team does this for a living, this is our lives and it hurts all of us equally. Michael was always philosophical about it. Spain, yes, it was a shame, we'd lost the race through it and we'd lost four points towards the championship. His attitude was "OK, that's the way it is."'

Symonds gives another example of Schumacher's sheer tenacity, what he calls a 'stunning example'. This was in Canada in 1995 on the journey to his second World Championship. 'We were leading that race by miles and we had a problem with the gearbox.' It was stuck in third. 'Michael came on the radio and said "OK, that's it, all over but I can get back to the pits." He got back to the pits, we managed to re-set the gearbox and he went out again. He'd been leading this race, obviously putting in quicker lap times than anyone else, and now he was nowhere' –

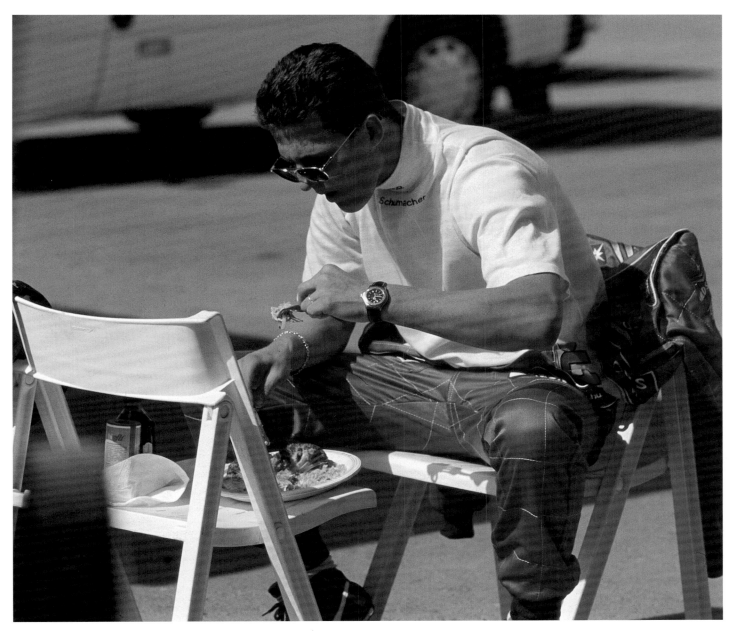

The moods of a test session . . . this one at Estoril. Schumacher plays football, Corinna in goal and the dog in central defence. At a Grand Prix you can eat like a banquet. In testing, you eat where you can.

seventh. 'He drove that car like there was no tomorrow. From that point on, his laps were just so much quicker than anyone else's and he got in the points. *That* is a mark of the great ones.'

As a matter of first principle, they drive as competitively as they can in all circumstances because they are made like that and, tactically, you never know. On lap 62 Gerhard Berger (Ferrari), sixth, made an ill-judged attempt to take Brundle (Ligier), fifth, and they were both out. It meant Schumacher inherited Brundle's position and the two points this brought. Championships have been won and lost on less.

That he finished the Canadian Grand Prix fifth, 44.676 seconds behind the winner, Alesi (Ferrari), was irrelevant.

By Spa in late August (when, incidentally, Schumacher's

move from Benetton to Ferrari had been confirmed), he led Hill 56–45. The weather wreaked its havoc, Hill qualifying eighth and Schumacher sixteenth. Symonds, wielding understatement again, describes this as 'interesting'. He explains that 'during qualifying on Saturday it was typical Spa, wet and drying out. Everything depended on one lap right at the end and we had a gearbox problem during qualifying – it started shifting of its own accord and Michael came on the radio and said "I've got a problem." I said "well, we'll finish the lap" – if you don't you're nowhere. He did finish the lap but was only on the eighth row of the grid.

'His attitude afterwards – bearing in mind that he's won the World Championship the year before and he's going for it again – was no hysterics, no throwing his toys out of the

The moods of 1993 . . . always plenty to look at in Monaco . . . Schumacher sprints back to get team-mate Riccardo Patrese's car for the final moments of qualifying at Silverstone after crashing his own. And yes, in Patrese's car he outqualified Patrese. Tracking Prost for the lead in Portugal (above), where Schumacher eventually took the win and Prost took the World Championship.

pram. In actual fact he was very light-hearted about it. Obviously we are professionals and we put just as much effort into it if we've qualified twentieth as we do when we're on pole. He thought "well, I've a bit more to do than I would have liked, but let's do it."'

Symonds sets out this attitude of mind. 'Michael was very good at working with the engineers in developing the car to get the best possible performance out of it and he'd work hard at that through Friday, through Saturday, but come Sunday he'd say "OK, that's what I've got to drive." He would almost switch his skills then. "This is actually what I have to race a Grand Prix in this afternoon so how can I get the best from it?"'

This is known as the art of the possible.

Crossing the line to complete the opening lap, Hill was up to sixth, Schumacher thirteenth. Into *La Source*, the Benetton wobbling under braking, he lunged inside Rubens Barrichello (Jordan) to be twelfth; Häkkinen spun – eleventh. Crossing the line, Schumacher was tenth (Hill fifth). Lap three – eighth some 8.8 seconds behind the leader, Alesi (Hill still fifth). Alesi pitted, Hill third and Schumacher seventh. Herbert, leading, spun and that let Hill through into second. Schumacher had reduced the gap to the new leader, Coulthard (Williams) to seven seconds. Herbert spun in the Bus Stop, balking Blundell (McLaren) – Schumacher fifth. At lap six, however, the gap to Coulthard was out to 9.4 seconds. Schumacher scythed past Irvine (Jordan) at the entrance to the Bus Stop – fourth. Schumacher set off after Berger and hauled him in, pressured him while, on lap 14, Coulthard toured with a gearbox problem – Hill now leading, Schumacher third.

Hill pitted a lap later, Berger following him so that Schumacher led. It had taken no more than 15 laps. Schumacher pitted on lap 18 and came out in second place. Soon enough the rain began and Hill pitted for wet tyres. Schumacher stayed out on dries.

Symonds has already spoken of the mutual respect between Schumacher and himself and explains that 'there were many instances of it' but adds 'we didn't always agree.

A deceptive study from 1993. Schumacher moves easily past Alain Prost (Williams) – but in qualifying! Damon Hill in the other Williams took pole anyway.

I don't think two strong people ever do. There was a classic case at Spa when we were racing Hill for the championship. Basically Michael was out on dry tyres and Damon came in for wet tyres, which I didn't necessarily think was the correct thing to do. We were leading the race and what we had to do was make sure that we got it right: didn't matter if we were a bit slower as long as we made the right decision. We had a discussion about it on the radio and Michael was pretty adamant he wanted to stay on the dry tyres.'

Out on the circuit Schumacher had Hill directly behind him and in theory Hill ought to have breezed by, but Schumacher demonstrated what someone called ruthlessness as he repeatedly blocked Hill – although to be able to do that with dry tyres on a track surface like ice was breathtaking. Hill was angered by the former and impressed by the latter.

'To me it was a risk assessment situation,' says Symonds. 'That assessment was that if we went onto wet tyres we would win the race, if we stayed on dry tyres and it was the right thing to do, we'd win the race by more – but if we stayed on dry tyres and it was the wrong thing to do, we'd lose the race. So it was absolutely obvious. Normally with the rules of engagement that we run at Benetton, the change from dry to wet tyres is the driver's decision [as we've seen] but in this case I over-ruled it. I said "no, we're going onto wet tyres." We had a bit of a discussion about it until finally – because I thought we were wasting time – I commanded him, if you like, on the radio that he had to come in for wet tyres. In he came and changed to wet tyres."'

He did not lose the lead during this pit stop – the Safety Car was out, and Hill came in too – and he won the race by 19.493 seconds. Afterwards Schumacher said to Symonds, "yes, I could tell from your voice that you meant what you said, and I could also tell that you know how to talk to children!"'

Schumacher joined Ferrari and, although in 1996 he was able to conjure three victories, he needed a formidable team behind him.

NOTE
[1] Feathering, as in applying a light touch to the accelerator pedal rather than pressing it full down for maximum power and speed.

Facts of the matter

As a graphic way of illustrating Schumacher's performance when stuck in fifth gear at Barcelona in 1994, here are his lap times from the TAG-Heuer timing system. They prove, in the cold way statistics do, that he was able to run at virtually the same pace before and after. Remember that the gearbox started to misbehave around lap 23.

Lap	Time		Lap	Time
Lap 1	1:30.840		Lap 34	1:27.576
Lap 2	1:26.971		Lap 35	1:27.674
Lap 3	1:26.552		Lap 36	1:27.061
Lap 4	1:26.462		Lap 37	1:28.687
Lap 5	1:25.936		Lap 38	1:28.571
Lap 6	1:25.709		Lap 39	1:26.340
Lap 7	1:25.713		Lap 40	1:26.171
Lap 8	1:25.597		Lap 41	1:26.884
Lap 9	1:27.542		Lap 42	1:28.140
Lap 10	1:25.553		Lap 43	1:32.870
Lap 11	1:25.768		Lap 44	1:28.050
Lap 12	1:27.202		Lap 45	1:34.742 *(pit)*
Lap 13	1:25.608		Lap 46	1:52.749
Lap 14	1:27.214		Lap 47	1:27.950
Lap 15	1:25.770		Lap 48	1:27.468
Lap 16	1:26.341		Lap 49	1:27.720
Lap 17	1:25.694		Lap 50	1:28.066
Lap 18	1:25.155		Lap 51	1:27.882
Lap 19	1:26.009		Lap 52	1:27.514
Lap 20	1:27.732		Lap 53	1:26.983
Lap 21	1:37.326 *(pit)*		Lap 54	1:27.202
Lap 22	2:02.829		Lap 55	1:28.802
Lap 23	1:31.835		Lap 56	1:28.803
Lap 24	1:31.503		Lap 57	1:27.896
Lap 25	1:29.368		Lap 58	1:28.297
Lap 26	1:30.282		Lap 59	1:28.873
Lap 27	1:29.634		Lap 60	1:28.853
Lap 28	1:28.438		Lap 61	1:31.903
Lap 29	1:28.740		Lap 62	1:30.877
Lap 30	1:27.970		Lap 63	1:32.240
Lap 31	1:27.129		Lap 64	1:31.417
Lap 32	1:27.277		Lap 65	1:35.387
Lap 33	1:27.193			

The winner, born to it, doing it, loving it (top). This is the aftermath of Belgium 1995. There may be trouble ahead. With Benetton just a memory, Schumacher went all out to win the championship for Ferrari. Here at Jerez in 1997 (above) he handles a Press Conference with rival Jacques Villeneuve. On the track they crashed and there it is on the big screen for all to see (right).

Chapter Five

TIME
TEAM

A question to Jody Scheckter who, for two decades, had a phrase attached to him like a billboard: 'last man to win the World Championship in a Ferrari'.

After 1979, was it necessary for Ferrari to shed some passion and hire pragmatic Anglo-Saxons to win the championship again, because they were competing against pragmatic Anglo-Saxon teams?

'They did, and it was no good for many years.'

This is a reference to Dr Harvey Postlethwaite and John Barnard, who both designed Ferraris which did not win the World Championship. It also introduces the idea that making Ferrari a successful team again was no simple matter, because Postlethwaite and Barnard both knew their business and had had significant successes of their own.

Looking back, it is difficult to comprehend the size of the problems Luca di Montezemolo inherited when he became Ferrari President in November 1991, with a brief to turn round the production car company and the Formula 1 team. He would do more than fulfil his brief. He'd create a culture within the company which, based on absolute excellence, led logically to Schumacher and Hungary and Suzuka in 2001.

Enzo Ferrari died in 1988. Although the team finished second in the Constructors' title that year they slipped to third in 1989 (drivers Nigel Mansell and Gerhard Berger), rallied to second in 1990 (Mansell and Alain Prost), were third again in 1991 (Prost, Jean Alesi, and Gianni Morbidelli). The team looked to be without discipline or direction, possibly beyond salvation except as a wonderful but increasingly irrelevant adornment to Formula 1 racing. As if to emphasise that, Prost – who'd arrived as the saviour – was fired after the 1991 Japanese Grand Prix on 20 October. Morbidelli, a journeyman, replaced him for the

Shooting range in South Africa, 1992.

Australian Grand Prix on 3 November. Di Montezemolo arrived at Maranello 12 days later.

CURRICULUM VITAE: The Marquis Luca Cordero di Montezemolo, born 31 August 1947, Bologna. Studied commercial law in Rome and attended Columbia University, New York. Joined the Lancia rally team, joined Ferrari in 1973. Took the team to championships with Niki Lauda in 1975, 1977. Promoted within the Fiat organisation (which owned Ferrari), becoming managing director of Cinzano, the drinks company, in 1984. From 1985 to 1990 was general manager of the World Soccer Cup held in Italy in 1990. Then Ferrari rang again.

While Ferrari invested some $80 million on re-tooling the production car base, and hiring personnel regardless of nationality, the Formula 1 team sank to fourth in 1992 (Alesi, Ivan Capelli and Nicola Larini) with 21 points against the 164 of Williams. Ferrari did not win a race in 1991 or 1992. Moreover the production cars sold only 2,289 in 1993 – it had been closer to 5,000 in the 1980s – and Ferrari were losing a fortune. Di Montezemolo's revolution would take time.

Screen star, Brazil, 1995 . . . Rory Byrne (left), the quiet man who designed master- pieces . . . Luca di Montezemolo (right), the man who spread out the vision and made it come true.

On 1 July 1993 Ferrari announced that Jean Todt would become Sporting Director, essentially running the Formula 1 effort. He had a background in rallying, and criticism rained down on di Montezemolo's decision to hire him. *Todt is French! Todt doesn't know anything about F1! Todt only knows about rallies!*

That wasn't the point, of course. Todt, a small, neat, fussy man, had worked in the Peugeot organisation where he ran their motorsport and was known as 'can do'. He was organised, understood other modern men, and was once quoted as saying that he 'liked to convince people' that they wanted to work with him. He also understood the mechanisms and nuances of creating and maintaining a team. He had done that with outstanding success in rallying.

CURRICULUM VITAE: Jean Todt, born 25 February 1946, Pierrefort (a tiny place near France's Massif Central). His father was a doctor but Todt wasn't interested in joining a profession – he intended to be a 'great' motorsport champion. It didn't happen. At 20 he was a co-driver (navigator) in rallying and remained active for 15 years. He created Peugeot Talbot Sport to contest World Rallying with the Peugeot 205 Turbo – it won a clutch of titles. He took Peugeot into the World Sports Car Championship but early in 1993 Peugeot made a decision not to manufacture a Formula 1 engine and chassis. Then di Montezemolo rang.

Todt would quickly realise the scale of what faced him, however much he savoured taking it on. He described Ferrari as a 'mythical team' and pointed out that he had loved racing all his life and the fact that he hadn't 'done' Formula 1 only made him more anxious to measure himself against it. In an interview with the *International Herald Tribune* he said there were 'lots of great sides' to his decision.

Years later he'd confess that often enough mighty Ferrari found itself 'fighting with very poor little teams' – reduced in the races to running against those from the back of the grid – and in those days just winning a point was a dream rather than an expectation. In Todt's first full season, 1994 (Alesi, Berger, Larini), they were a distant third in the Constructors' title with three pole positions and a solitary win. At Benetton, young Michael Schumacher was winning the championship with six pole positions and eight wins, although he shared the credit with a South African, Rory Byrne, who supervised the design of the car, and an Englishman, Ross Brawn, who supervised everything else.

Todt did inherit some people you'd need as pillars of any edifice, among them Nigel Stepney who knew exactly what he was doing in the noise, chaos and confusion of the pit lane. I use Stepney as representative of those who, most of them anonymous, are pillars. If you go to any Grand Prix team headquarters you see them peering at computer screens or working in assembly bays. Often they do repetitive jobs.

Stepney was a mechanic and always had been (although he'd wanted to be a footballer). He'd worked with Senna at Lotus and – perhaps there, perhaps everywhere – had evolved a philosophy: *there is no point in being in motor racing, and going to the races, if you have no chance of winning.*

Stepney – solid, genial, experienced – was exactly the kind of man you could use as part of the foundation to construct a team which would win.

CURRICULUM VITAE: Nigel Stepney, born 14 November 1958, Ufton, Warwickshire. Became an apprentice mechanic with a Coventry racing team, Broadspeed, moving to Shadow in Formula 1 in 1979. Elio de Angelis was driving there and when he went to Lotus the following season Stepney went too. He stayed until 1988, joining Benetton and then, in 1991, ran Nelson Piquet's F3000 team. Barnard took him to Maranello in order – no doubt – to bring English pragmatism with him.

In 1993, at Donington, I espied Stepney coming across the paddock on a moped. As he passed me I called out 'is it all true?' and, grinning enormously, he shouted 'yes!' and sped on. I didn't have to specify that I was talking about one aspect of Ferrari which wasn't mythical: the endemic politics and the boiling temperaments. Todt was, though, beginning to bring that under some sort of management structure.

CURRICULUM VITAE: Paolo Martinelli, born 26 September 1952, Modena, Italy. In 1977 got a degree in mechanical engineering from Bologna University and joined Ferrari; then joined the Ferrari Formula 1 department on 'the first day of 1995'. Since then, has worked with engine designer Gilles Simon, widely acknowledged as giving the Ferrari cars power and reliability.

In 1995, while young Michael Schumacher was taking his second championship – four poles, nine wins, and Benetton (Brawn and Byrne prominent) were taking the Constructors' title – Ferrari (Alesi and Berger) had one pole and one win. Jean Todt reached for his telephone. . . .

The man Todt hired brought with him a whole array of strengths which he had finessed into a whole. He would become the highest-paid driver the world had ever seen and, however hard it would be to believe, was good value for money. Todt offered Schumacher more than $20 million per annum and Schumacher said yes.

Gary Anderson, who still speaks about Schumacher's début with Jordan in terms of reverence, has watched his subsequent career with close interest. He sets out glimpses of what Ferrari would be getting for the money.

'One year Michael had pole but the Ferrari wasn't quick enough on the straights for the race, so he said to take wing off.[1] The second section of the circuit was all about driving, not speed, and without the wing he'd lose the downforce but he said "that's my problem. I'll handle that bit – what I can't do anything about is the straight line speed."

'In 1995, Eddie Irvine said at Silverstone before he went to Ferrari "give me the same car as Michael Schumacher and I can beat him." I said "Eddie, Eddie, no way as long as you've got a hole in your behind, but I really hope you get the opportunity to find out." I worked with Eddie at Jaguar when he left Ferrari and his comment was "Michael is the best of all, full stop. Nobody's in the same league." In all four years of Eddie at Ferrari his average was eight-tenths slower in the race and nine-tenths slower in qualifying. When the car was bad the gap was much bigger but as the car got good it was closer. Michael was able to drive the bad car better. The guys who're all right in a good car can do a good job, but they don't "make" the car – Michael makes the car.'

Schumacher was Todt's great coup. Schumacher was far more than a leading driver, Schumacher was a team builder. 'At the time I came to Ferrari,' he would say, 'it was clear that it was not only a driver that was missing, it was the technical people missing.'

Martinelli, of course, was already in place. 'I was there when Michael arrived. I didn't know him personally before that – I made his acquaintance when he joined Ferrari. I had an image of him from his career up to then, very fast. My first impression? That he was kind, polite and strong-minded. He had a strong attitude to support anyone on the team towards the goal: try to improve, try to make the best car, try to win.'

During 1996, as Schumacher settled in and – almost by willpower – made the Ferrari win three times, Brawn's phone rang. . . .

Brawn was coy (to me) about how much influence

The world likes to gaze at Schumacher . . . Jerez, 1997 (top), explaining the crash with Villeneuve? Rush hour, Buenos Aires, 1998 (below).

Schumacher had wielded to get him to Maranello, contenting himself with the most diplomatic explanation that they seemed to have worked well together at Benetton.

CURRICULUM VITAE: Ross Brawn, born 23 November 1954, Manchester. Engineering apprentice at the Atomic Energy Research Establishment, Harwell, where he worked for five years. Joined Williams R & D in 1976, working on the installation of a wind tunnel. Joined Arrows as Chief Designer, Arrows were fourth in the Constructors' title in 1988. He joined Tom Walkinshaw and worked on sports cars (they won the 1991 World Championship). As joint team principal at Benetton with Flavio Briatore, Walkinshaw brought Brawn there. Seeing that Schumacher hadn't actually signed with Jordan, he brought him there too, at the end of 1991. The partnership went as far back as that, and as deep as that.

Rory Byrne, meanwhile, had retreated to Thailand where he intended to start a scuba-diving school. He had always wanted to do that and felt he had achieved as much as he could in Formula 1. After all, Benetton – only in existence since 1986 – had defeated the major teams, Ferrari and McLaren and Williams. Byrne's decision was so final that he left virtually nobody but Brawn a contact number, and only did that so Brawn could (literally) drop in if he was ever passing that way.

... The crowd watching the drivers watching the crowd at the Hungaroring, 1998.

In January 1997 the new car was being tested at Fiorano, the Ferrari test track, and Brawn watched with mounting apprehension. During subsequent testing at Jerez, Barnard, who had designed the car, departed for good. Brawn gave Todt the number Byrne had left, and Todt reached for his telephone. It rang on an island to the south of Thailand. Byrne's landlady rushed out shouting 'call for you!' and Byrne thought it must be a family crisis. When he reached the receiver he heard the cultivated French tones of Jean Todt. . . .

CURRICULUM VITAE: Rory Byrne, born 10 January 1944, Pretoria. Got a BSc in industrial chemistry at university in Johannesburg ('I had to learn engineering myself!') and designed model gliders. Worked importing, making and selling things which made cars go faster. Came

to England in 1973 with a friend in Formula Ford 1600. In 1977 he met the people running Toleman, who had designs on Formula 1, and reached it in 1981. Toleman became Benetton in 1986.

The team was in place now, specifically: di Montezemolo, President; Todt, Sporting Director; Brawn, Technical Director; Byrne, Chief Designer; Martinelli, Engine Director; Gilles Simon, Engine Designer; Stepney, Team Co-ordinator who in 2001 would become Manager.

Any team, particularly if it is multi-national and spends the whole of its existence in fierce combat on a global stage – its fate always decided by fractions of a second – must be a curious creature full of exaggerated strengths and sometimes not very well concealed weaknesses. Ferrari had long been crippled by internal tensions and a sort of divine Italian madness. Years before, Alain Prost had summed it up in a phrase. Whenever Ferrari win a race, he said, there is a crisis of optimism. And Scheckter, who partnered Gilles Villeneuve at Ferrari, said that when Villeneuve reached Maranello and 'came flying into the carpark at the factory he would do a 360-degree wheelspin and the mechanics would all cheer'.[2]

Now what they were getting was proven French organisational flair, Anglo-Saxon discipline and Germanic thoroughness. Neither Ferrari nor the world would be the same again.

Brawn and Byrne had worked together since 1991 and, as Byrne has recounted, when they first met they 'talked for a couple of hours, shook hands and that was it'.[3] In 1996, when they were both still with Benetton, Byrne would say: 'One of the secrets of the company's success is how well I get on with Ross. We see eye-to-eye on virtually every issue. We very seldom disagree to a point where we have to make a fundamental decision on the way we go – his or mine. Ross is a proper Technical Director, setting procedures, establishing systems, race engineering and overall engineering programmes.'[4]

The partnership simply continued at Ferrari.

Brawn's management style was, in his own description, 'walking quietly with a big stick' and setting an example. 'You can't have a tantrum. You can't lose control and expect the people who work for you not to do the same.'[5]

Stepney has a philosophy, taught to him early on in his career by a chief mechanic: *think through what you do before it happens*. He'd keep doing that and tell the mechanics around him to do it too.

Stepney was responsible for getting the equipment and parts, estimated at 55,000lbs, to each race and co-ordinating the pit stops, now arguably the crux and the crucible of the races. These pit stops involve 20 men and Stepney rotates them so that if one is injured another can take his place (although Stepney himself fell victim to a lack

Opposite: Horsepower whispers as Ross Brawn outlines masterpieces of movement (left and middle). Maybe. Or they could be just enjoying themselves. The team-builder must understand communal morale (opposite right). Malaysia, 2000, and many at Ferrari looked as wonderfully silly. The team (above), though mercifully not all with hair-pieces.

of co-ordination in Spain in 2000 when, holding the fuel nozzle into Schumacher's car, he was thrown to the ground and his ankle broken as, mistakenly, Schumacher was given the signal to go).

It wasn't Schumacher's fault and Stepney pays tribute to how easy Schumacher makes it for the pit crew waiting with tyres and fuel. He stops in a 'perfect position' 99% of the time, and that makes the crew confident he'll stop *exactly* where they need him to.

Todt expresses his philosophy in a French proverb: *only mediocre people fulfil their full potential, high level people can always improve*. He would say firmly (in 1991) 'I feel that we have a very good team. I am proud of the people I've gathered around me. I like the people, I trust them at all levels.' And, on how he works: 'I want to make sure that things that have to be done the same day are done. It's energy-consuming, nerve-consuming, head-consuming, whatever, but that's the way it is. I need to be a catalyst if people need to be pushed but very often they push themselves.'[6]

There were troubles ahead, like in San Marino and Canada, 1999.

Schumacher, as Brawn attests, is a team player who keeps any problems within the team and searches for solutions within the team.

Schumacher, Brawn adds, is hard and if the car isn't right he lets Brawn know all about it. Brawn appreciates the strength of this approach. No doubt the whole team appreciated Schumacher's words over the radio after he'd won the 2001 championship at the Hungaroring. 'It's so lovely to work with you guys. I love you all, I love you all, thank you.'

Martinelli, reviewing how the Time Team was created and how it began to function, says 'we have made continuous progress since the arrival of Jean Todt. You can certainly say that if you consider the steps forward since 1993: only one win in '94, only one win in '95, three wins in '96 etc etc so we have been improving year by year.'

It seems there has been a discipline in the whole team which did not exist before.

'Honestly, I think you have to start from Mr di Montezemolo – the merit came from him and Jean Todt. They have been able to organise a strong team in every area, because it cannot be just a driver alone – even if he is the best driver in Formula 1, like Michael. He cannot win if he does not have a car at a good level, an engine at a good level and so on. So we tried to improve step by step in every area and we also passed through a difficult period [the early 1990s], and I think the strength of the team has been improved by those difficulties. When you are in trouble you have to react, you have to work hard and you create a spirit: that spirit is a positive attitude by everybody.'

But one thing that everybody says about Schumacher is that he is a team player.

'Absolutely. You get everything from him, that's absolutely true. He is very focused on priorities, which are the necessary steps on any area of the vehicle. Of course I speak mainly about the engine. Michael is able to be very clever when he is doing laps in the car: which are the points that must be addressed first? He understands time, also. Normally with an engine if you have to make a modification of a component it can require not just a few seconds or hours but sometimes weeks. Of course with our racing engineer Mr D'Agostino [Giuseppe D'Agostino, Production and Chief Track Engineer], with all the designers, also sometimes we make some meetings – we have a strong chief designer of the engine, Gilles Simon. Michael is able to motivate but also to illustrate properly to the relevant people which are the topics which must be addressed.'

Is Schumacher interested in engines?

'Of course. He's very technically curious and he understands his responsibilities and what we as engineers can do, so it's a combination. He says "OK, here is a problem, you have to focus on it, you have to react." What is the critical area? Michael is very clever. He says "OK, in corners 3, 4, 5 this area of revs must be improved" – or maybe it'll be another area. This means that sometimes we can operate in a very quick way because we have very precise indications.'

Is Schumacher hard on engines?

'He is correct – he is demanding towards the engine because he's fast! You cannot be soft while using a Formula 1

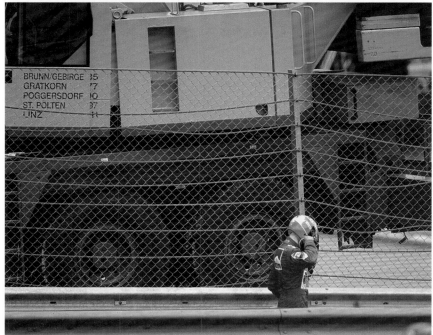

The moods of the championship, 2000 . . . The start in Australia (left above) and the McLarens have already gone out of reach. On his own at Melbourne (left below) and, as the McLarens broke down, taking the win. Mayhem in Austria (above), with cars bumping through the first corner where Schumacher, touched by Ricardo Zonta's BAR and hit by Jarno Trulli's Jordan, was halted. Nothing he could do (right) but make his way back to the pits . . .

engine! When I say correct, he is very correct in his use of the engine at the top of its potential: never too much. Sometimes when we have – rarely, we can say – a reliability issue it is only due to our failure, not to him. I can put it like this: no driver abuse of engine. As you know, the best way to achieve something in motor racing is with two pedals – one for acceleration, the other for braking. . . .'

Todt, speaking after the Hungaroring in 2001, said 'for me, Schumacher is like a son, a brother, a member of the family.' Todt had said in 1999 'Michael's a great driver, a great guy. We have a group of individuals who get on very well professionally and socially, which is very important. Michael is totally committed to the team as a driver.'[7]

Irvine, Schumacher's team-mate at Ferrari from 1996 to 1999, passed his own judgement to me[8] when he said 'with Todt and Ross I learnt how a Formula 1 team should run.

. . . Hockenheim was just as bad after Schumacher and Giancarlo Fisichella (Benetton) crashed into the first corner.

Rory delivered the car to Ross and Ross ran the show. That's pretty much the way it works.' Todt, of course, was unobtrusive in the sense that he drew the whole effort together; Brawn could not help but be obtrusive because he was making the tactical decisions which, with Schumacher implementing them, fascinated the global audience.

Scheckter insists that 'Schumacher's contribution has been very important to Ferrari. I have always said that he pulled the team together and many great drivers do that.'

Jackie Stewart feels that it was 'Schumacher's ability to bring that team together' which was decisive, and adds that 'at the end of the day he is the captain of the ship. No matter what di Montezemolo does, no matter how good Jean Todt is, no matter how brilliant Ross Brawn, no matter how clever Rory Byrne is, the one thing that has brought this to pass is that they all want to work for Schumacher and they all know that, given what they can provide, he will deliver. That's why they don't want to leave. If you were to go and say to Ross Brawn right now "come and work for me" he'd say "why should I work for you when I'm working for Michael Schumacher? Who's going to bring me that level of success?"

'What Schumacher has got there is a great band of real experts who'll stay – short of a few of them getting tired and leaving, like Jean Todt. Rory could too, because he's retired or tried to retire a couple of times. Ross might get tired of living in Italy. The point, however, is that for the period of time Schumacher wants to continue at that end of the business, he has enough time to win at least one more World Championship, if not two, and the great band may well stay together.'

Stewart adds this intriguing footnote. 'Schumacher has much more authority in Ferrari than Senna would ever have had. Ron Dennis totally controls McLaren, Jean Todt doesn't at Ferrari. He's an employee. Ken Tyrrell controlled his own team. Colin Chapman controlled his own team. John Cooper controlled his own team.'

The received wisdom within Formula 1 – and this goes right back to the beginning in 1950 – is that you need strong, almost dictatorial men to run it properly. They listen, they consult, they discuss, then they and they alone decide. It works for running the whole thing (Max Mosley at the FIA, Bernie Ecclestone at FOCA) and it works for running the teams (Dennis, Sir Frank Williams, Jordan, Walkinshaw, Sauber). I wonder if the real achievement at Ferrari has been to contradict this received wisdom and triumph using a corporate structure? That might just be Michael Schumacher's real triumph too: leading a team to contradict history itself.

NOTES

[1] Taking some wing off reduces the downforce and enables the car to go faster in straight lines but is an obvious disadvantage in corners where, with less downforce, you get less grip.

[2] *Gilles Villeneuve: The Life of the Legendary Racing Driver* by Gerald Donaldson (MRP, 1989).

[3] Tifosi Club website.

[4] Gran Com website.

[5] *F1 Racing* magazine.

[6] The Atlas F1 website.

[7] Ibid.

[8] *Inside the Mind of the Grand Prix Driver* (Haynes, 2001).

Facts of the matter

Cumulatively this is how the Ferrari Formula 1 team was reborn and then nurtured to the point where, by 2001, people spoke quite naturally of living in The Ferrari Era:

	Poles	Wins	C'tors' position	Drivers' champ titles	Points
1990	3	6	2	0	110
1991	0	0	3	0	55.5
Arrival of di Montezemolo					
1992	0	0	4	0	21
Arrival of Todt					
1993	0	0	4	0	28
1994	3	1	3	0	71
Arrival of Martinelli					
1995	1	1	3	0	73
Arrival of Schumacher, Brawn					
1996	4	3	2	0	70
Arrival of Byrne					
1997	3	5	2	0	102
1998	3	6	2	0	133
1999	3	6	1	0	128
2000	10	10	1	1	170
2001	11	9	1	1	179

Nigel Stepney ruminates on the Time Team and Schumacher. 'I know it's a team but we have all our eggs in one basket and without Michael . . . well, if you think of when Senna left McLaren, McLaren just disappeared. Same at Lotus. It's a very high risk not to have two baskets. When Michael had his accident [at Silverstone in 1999] we had Eddie Irvine and Eddie raised his level. Eddie was fighting for the championship, his level's raised – but it wasn't at the same level as Michael. When Michael came back that season he basically destroyed everybody. We learnt that if a driver has a break' – no pun intended – 'and relaxes, when he comes back he performs a lot better!

'We have a very good balance in the team generally. Everybody knows their position and nobody has any need to be negative. Everybody is doing the best they can in their area. So, OK, you always try to improve but we try to improve as a group and have confidence in the people around us to try and improve as well. We try not to change people like at Ferrari years ago when it was very unstable: you changed one person and all the people underneath changed too. It was an instability problem. Now we work in a very stable atmosphere. I was here before Todt and Ross so I survived some of the . . . [chuckle] . . . other days. Now you have a group of people but if you lose that group of people in three years I hate to think what will happen.

'The main thing is to keep up the performance. I thought after we had won the championship double once – constructors' and drivers' – what motivation have I got to win the double again? In actual fact to win it this year [2001] was better than last year because we proved it wasn't a fluke, we proved we want to go on and win more and more.'

Isn't that like certain drivers who win a World Championship and think 'I've done it' – Damon Hill, Mansell, Hunt – and other drivers like Ayrton and Michael think 'I've won one, I'm going to do this again and again'?

'That's right. You think about why you want to carry on, what motivation you've got, then you just think *it's so good to win, to be on top of everybody.*

'Michael is very professional, a very good person. Don't get me wrong: I have great respect for him too. It's not easy to work with drivers that aren't at the same level as him. That's the hardest thing. After working with Senna and Michael it's hard to accept drivers at a lower level who can't perform even when they've got the same equipment. It's not a case of these drivers trying the best they can, it's a case of whether they've got it or not. The equipment we give them is all the same, and you can't argue the toss that it isn't. That's just an excuse and at the end of the day people only accept excuses for a short time: then – *now* – you have to deliver.'

Just as Schumacher delivers and delivers and delivers.

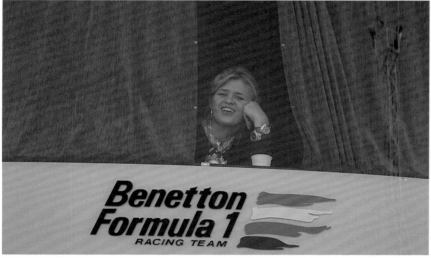

Husband and wife team. He wins races, like the 2000 Italian Grand Prix, while she guards the family jewels – her watch and his! – at Jerez in 1994.

Chapter Six

A TEAR FOR THE PAST

A hot and dry afternoon at Imola in 1983: on lap 55 of the San Marino Grand Prix, Riccardo Patrese forced his Brabham past the Ferrari of Patrick Tambay and took the lead. The moment proved too intoxicating for Patrese who plunged off into a tyre wall. As he got out of the Brabham the crowd roared their approval – approval that he'd crashed, giving the lead back to the Ferrari. The fact that Patrese was Italian and Tambay was French mattered nothing to the Italian crowd. What did matter was Ferrari.

Tambay duly brought the Ferrari home to victory although it stopped on the slowing down lap and the crowd climbed over the barriers, swarmed the car and lifted him out of it. He had to be rescued by the police. Later he'd say it had been the most emotional day of his career, adding: 'You know, to win here in Ferrari number 27 . . . it's difficult for me to put it into words but I hope everyone understands that what happened today was more than just winning a race. Something incredible.'

The 27 Ferrari had been the one in which Gilles Villeneuve was killed a year before. Villeneuve was already a mythical figure within Ferrari. Tambay was godfather to Gilles' son Jacques.

Tambay's Ferrari (the 126 C2/B) was a beautiful car and, like so many in the turbo era, ferociously fast. In qualifying he'd averaged 197.288kmh (122mph) round Imola's twists and turns, and still only been third on the grid.

Michael Schumacher knew nothing about this sort of thing because the past did not interest him. Tambay remembers meeting him in Japan at the end of his first racing season – 1991 – and introducing himself. 'He didn't have a clue who I was or what I had done. He didn't know

I'd been a racing driver. I was just an old guy who was trying maybe to get an autograph from him. That's the feeling I had then.'

Stéphane Samson, a French journalist, had an idea. 'I am a friend of Tambay and he was always explaining how this particular race – Imola '83 – was for him. I felt it would be wonderful to have Patrick, so passionate about Ferrari, and Michael who didn't seem to care at all – just the opposite of Patrick, very rational – together, and to have Michael drive the car.' This was the spring of 1999, and no Ferrari had won at Imola since Tambay.

When it was arranged, the day would assume several degrees of importance, not least because of Schumacher's reaction to the car. It was one of the rare occasions when he has driven such a car and it afforded a glimpse – no more – of what he might have done if his career had been then. There is always a question of how, overall, a judgement can be made on the relative abilities of the greatest drivers.

The Ferrari turbo in 1983, with Patrick Tambay driving it.

Versatility *must* be a factor.

Once upon a time the turbo car belonged to Tambay but 'we had a family feud, what you call a divorce. My wife's lawyers wanted to saw the thing in two and I didn't know if they wanted the front part or the back part! It had to go to an auction and it was bought by a friend of mine. He owns the car and he's run it at Goodwood[1] a couple of times. He very kindly loaned it to us for that one test.'

Samson emphasises that Schumacher 'doesn't have any historical background from Formula 1, he doesn't know anything about what happened in the 1970s or even in the 1980s. That was part of the contract we had with Michael's PR: *just don't ask him any questions about the history of the sport because he doesn't know and he doesn't care.* Apparently when he got to Ferrari he didn't know anything about the legend and he just wanted to drive for them.'

So, that spring day, the 126 was taken to Fiorano, Ferrari's test track, where Schumacher would be testing the current car, the F399. Tambay, stocky in middle age and with wisps of white threaded into his sideburns, stood lost in contemplation as it was unloaded from the transporter at 7.30am. Some of the mechanics who'd worked on it in '83 were there too.

'It was the exact chassis that won at Imola and a very emotional day because it was the first time that Patrick had gone back to Fiorano since his Ferrari days [Tambay left Ferrari at the end of 1983, joining Renault]. He had never been there since – and that race had been very strange for Patrick, because he is convinced he wasn't alone in the cockpit. He still feels that Gilles was with him, helping him,' Samson says.

In the background Schumacher hammered round and round in the F399 and, as Samson explains, 'between two runs he came to look at it. He waited until everyone was more or less away from the car, then he went around it and looked at it very carefully examining the details, trying to understand how it was working, what the exact suspension geometry was. He asked Patrick questions. I think that was, first, to understand how the car had been designed. He was very surprised to see where the radiators were – on the side pods – and very surprised by how big the wings were. I think that was second, because he wanted to check if it had been really well maintained.

'He was trying to draw confidence from this car, trying to see if he'd be able to push with it and have fun. He told me he was a bit scared when he had to drive a very old car because he always felt something could break on them. I think he was more concerned about any possibility of hurting himself than about damage to the car, although I imagine that in 1983 the drivers thought it was the best possible in terms of security!' (They did, but with great reservations, as we'll see in a moment.)

He asked Tambay how much horsepower the 126 had, and when Tambay said 1200 in qualifying and 900 in the races Schumacher said 'wow!' He asked if the pedals really were ahead of the front axle and Tambay nodded. He asked if there was anything to protect the driver's legs – it seemed they touched the suspension. Tambay said yes, they did touch it.

'That,' Schumacher concluded instantly, 'is fantastically dangerous.'

(Samson remembers clearly that Schumacher 'noticed the steering arms were more or less at the end of your legs. If he had to avoid something, and he hit the wall or the tyres, it would really be a problem for his legs. He wasn't scared for himself [in the sense of driver error] because he knew exactly what he was going to do with the car but he said once again what he always says: *I think I wouldn't have been able to race in those days. It was too dangerous and I wouldn't be interested in doing a race with such a car*'.)

Tambay remembers 'he came to me and he looked at me in a strange way. I had the feeling that he didn't really believe I could have been a works Ferrari driver. Initially he looked at the car like it was just another piece of equipment. Then he looked at me and asked "you did actually drive this?" Obviously I'd put on weight since 1983. He was a little bit condescending, if I may say so.'

Anyway, Tambay said he had driven it.

Schumacher: 'I never could have done that, it's not safe. You have the shock absorbers and the springs, they are inboard and just protected by a little padding. Obviously there are some holes in the tub and the water can come in. The feet are way, way upfront.'

Tambay is sure that Schumacher felt the regulations under which the cars of 1983 were built had not produced safety, something Tambay and the drivers of that time had felt too, and they'd done a lot of lobbying to get the feet behind the front axle.

Schumacher: 'I don't think I would have driven that.'

Tambay: 'Of course you would. It would have been part of your era and you would have driven it and you would have gone flat out with it.'

Schumacher: 'No, no, I'm not so sure.'

'It was very interesting,' Samson says, 'to see how Michael – who doesn't pay attention to any statistics or any strange stories – listened to Patrick explaining to him about that race before Michael tested the car himself. He was quite interested, a bit curious in a way, and I sensed he didn't know what to think. You could see that. He was a bit moved by what Patrick was saying: explaining his race and describing it in a lot of detail. The tears were not far away because Patrick was very emotional.

'Before, Michael had just felt that it was driving in an old car with a normal gearbox. I think he saw that as a bit of a pain to have to do at the beginning, but then he heard the explanations. It meant that he looked at the car and he didn't know what to expect and he didn't have any particular feelings about it, but once he had listened to Patrick and he understood what the car really *meant*, he began to be more interested in it. He measured a bit more what the Ferrari legend was and what it means to so many people. I wouldn't say Michael was shaken but I would say moved by the story Patrick was telling and then by Patrick's behaviour.'

The 126 was parked outside Enzo Ferrari's house – Ferrari had a house at the circuit, and it had a number, 27, just above the door. The engine was fired up, the turbo howling and gurgling, and Schumacher was fascinated by that. As the howling echoed from in front of Enzo's house for the first time since 1983, the emotion deepened.

Schumacher went back to the F399 and did his next run. Samson wrote: 'As the afternoon draws on, the sun floods the track with a beautiful orange light. At last the driver's day job is done, and he pulls into the pits.'

Tambay says 'we were there at 7.30 in the morning and the test happened at 9.30 in the evening, so we stood the whole day waiting for him to do his ten laps in it. I said "I hope you can get a little bit of the magic of that race in '83." Stéphane and I felt that a lot of things happened when he came close to the car. The wind started blowing, leaves were turning – strange things. Stéphane noticed this and we looked at one another and we said they *were* strange things.'

The mood of Suzuka, 2000 . . . Late evening and still the crowd is there, surrounding him.

Samson wrote: 'The 126 is pushed out and, spontaneously, the old mechanics burst into applause. They know they're about to witness something special. By contrast Schumacher seems almost shy, confused. For some of these guys this chassis is real life, real memories: for him it's history. He walks slowly over, then climbs aboard. He struggles to get his legs into the aluminium cockpit, because the steering column barks against his shins and calls for some contortion. Finally, he's sitting. He adjusts his rear-view mirrors – as if automatically – and then lightly lays his hands on the steering wheel. He slowly rocks it from lock to lock, his face an expression of delight.'

Tambay, stooping towards him, gives advice and points out that the turbo doesn't like to go below 5000 revs.

Samson remembers: 'I think the last time Michael drove a single-seater with a normal [manual] gearbox was maybe the Jordan or Benetton in 1991 – and the Ferrari gearbox from '83 couldn't be compared to the Benetton gearbox from 1991! Even when he put it into first gear to move away from the pits it was smooth, the revs held perfectly. He didn't stall, he didn't get away like a maniac with smoking rubber and wheels spinning. All the mechanics were crying. It was so emotional for them. Maybe Michael understood, looking into the eyes of those guys, maybe he understood what this symbolic thing of having him drive a number 27 for the first time at Fiorano meant.'

(An aside from Tambay: 'You have to have respect for every era, every car, every mechanic, every driver because it's part of their own histories and history itself. It was very intense memories that came up to the surface again.')

'Out he went, never a single problem to pass up to second gear, third, fourth. It was always waang, waang, waang – very smooth, very quick – and Patrick was impressed. He was very kind with the car. He pushed only after two or three laps when the engine was hot and everything was working very well. He'd spent those two or three laps judging the car and playing with it, warming the tyres. He made it go fast on the straights. I think he wanted to check what the acceleration was with such a turbo charged thing. He never really pushed in the corners, basically I think because he didn't really know where the car was coming from and there was a still a feeling of *un*safety. One wheel had too much grease on it and it began to smoke and he thought the car was on fire. He did five to eight quick laps but he was not completely confident.

'When he came in and jumped from the car he said that the gearbox was awful – although he hadn't made one mistake with it – and Patrick said it was strange to hear him say that because he thought it was a beautiful gearbox, the best gearbox he'd ever had!'

Tambay says 'yes, the gearbox was as nice as bread and butter! It was a pure marvel, a marvellous piece of equipment.'

Schumacher would say: 'Technically, to drive this car means resorting to systems which are no longer current. You have to brake with the right foot, use the clutch and the conventional gearbox which only has five gears.' He'd had an impression of 'fiddling' with the gear lever the whole time. 'I never knew if it had engaged or not.'

Tambay says that, to Schumacher, 'everything must have felt hopeless, the brakes, the engine because it's a turbo – with the big turbo lag and then bang – but, then, it was the best thing available.'

Samson remains convinced that Schumacher learnt more than how to handle another old car. 'Maybe it was one of those days when you make a step towards understanding.'

Tambay had ambivalent feelings about that, although he does say: 'No team is ordinary but Ferrari obviously is something different. Schumacher said that day that he would probably start collecting his own racing cars. He didn't know if he was going to drive them because he didn't know whether in a few years he would be interested in doing that. He said he didn't know if he would be interested in having his son drive or race.

'My son is now racing and I never thought that this would happen. You mature, you grow older and wiser but when you are a racing driver you can't afford to have those thoughts and those feelings. You must be a hard, tough, racing bastard if you want to be successful the way he is!'

Samson concludes: 'I would say if he had been racing in the 1980s he would have been able to handle that car, just looking at how he used the gearbox and car. You could see that the approach he had was very professional – looking at it first, trying to understand it first and then doing the two or three laps warming everything, checking the brakes, the steering. And the way he used the gearbox: Patrick couldn't believe how smooth but efficient Michael was with that gearbox, especially as he had never driven such a thing before.'

Before we leave this, which will have relevance in Chapters Nine and Ten, here is Martin Brundle driving the 1955 Mercedes Grand Prix car. Brundle partnered Schumacher at Benetton in 1992 and of all his team-mates ran him closest. Schumacher finished on 53 points, Brundle 38. Brundle drove the Mercedes at Spa in 1998.[2]

'It's the first time I've even sat in something like this and I really didn't know what to expect. You know the driving position is going to be odd because there is a huge gearbox bellhousing between your knees so the distance between the brake pedal and the clutch must be about two feet. It's a bit like the *Doctor Who* phone box, bigger on the inside than it looks from the outside. The bonnet seems very long. You feel, too, as if you are sitting on the car rather than in it and the mirrors are like on a motorcycle: all you can see is your own shoulders. Clearly they didn't pay much attention to what was going on behind them and later on I began to understand why. You had to concentrate so bloody hard on what was going on in front of you. Physically I found the car easy to drive but mentally it was incredibly hard.

'Changing gear: these days it's a matter of 20 milliseconds, a flick of your index finger, but on this car it's a very conscious thing. You blip, you place the lever, you push it all very deliberately. I really had to concentrate. It's quite easy, for example, to go from fifth to second which fortunately I didn't do because I imagine that would have given the engine a bit of a hurry-up.

'As far as handling was concerned, the car turned in quite nicely and the basic balance was good although there were some curious loads coming through the steering wheel. In medium speed corners like *Les Combes* you could place the car more or less where you wanted it. What about the brakes? Well, because I brake quite early for *Les Combes* anyway, at first I didn't grasp that it doesn't slow down very well, although funnily enough it seems to depend on which corner you are in and how fast you are going. Coming in to the Bus Stop, for example, it didn't seem to want to slow at all.

'I was supposed to be keeping pace with the Safety Car, and that was a special 5.5 litre Merc CLK with Jochen Mass[3] driving it: a quick car, a very quick car. And Jochen was pushing very hard, apparently, but he couldn't keep up with me. To be honest I didn't think I was going that fast but then I began to realise this car must be quite slippery through the air. I was doing 150mph through the kinks before *Blanchimont*.[4] It was at this point that I began to think about the absence of seat belts, rollover bars and the like. I began to look around and think *if you were going to hit something, what would you do?* In a modern car if you're going to crash you make sure you do certain things beforehand but with this one I really had no idea what I'd do.

'I didn't slow down because I was enjoying it so much but I did begin to feel nervous in the high-speed corners

The moods of Suzuka 2000 . . . The pits were sombre at times. . . . Practise makes perfect for the team too . . . Corinna and Schumacher's manager Willy Weber find a moment of solitude at the back of the Ferrari pit . . . The tacticians, getting it right.

because occasionally the car seemed to have a mind of its own. It was rather like flying a helicopter – that sense that if you ever let anything develop you'll have a hell of a job getting it back again. In the back of a modern Formula 1 driver's mind is the acceptance that he might get hurt doing this but it never enters your mind that you might get killed. Back then, that thought must have been right at the front of your mind and very much part of your decision-making process.

'I didn't know what to expect from this car. In terms of power perhaps it wasn't as fast as I anticipated but I had to keep reminding myself it was 44 years old and only two and a half litres. In every other way, though, I came out of it with even higher respect for the drivers of those days. I've been round the old Spa where they raced it and it is unbelievable to think they took Formula 1 cars round there. When you try and put that together with what you felt in the car . . . Jesus Christ.'

Degrees of importance: whatever Schumacher felt about the turbo car, and Brundle felt about the 1955 Mercedes, they adapted to them almost instantly and could make them go a bit. Who can say they wouldn't have been able to do that with any car ever made? Just like Fangio, Moss and Clark did.

NOTES

[1] The Goodwood Festival of Speed, featuring cars of historical significance, is held in West Sussex, England, every summer.
[2] Interview by Nigel Roebuck, used with kind permission.
[3] Jochen Mass, incidentally, had been a tutor to Schumacher, Wendlinger and Frentzen when they came into sports cars with Mercedes, partnering each of them in the races. He refers to them as the kids, and thoroughly enjoyed the whole thing.
[4] In the car's sister, Juan-Manuel Fangio did the fastest lap of the 1955 Belgian Grand Prix on the old, full Spa – a road circuit with virtually no protection – averaging 195kmh/121mph, and won the race at an average speed of 191kmh/118mph. In the car itself Stirling Moss finished eight seconds behind Fangio.

Facts of the matter

On 1 May 1983, Patrick Tambay started third on the grid and covered 60 laps (302 kilometres) in 1h 37m 52.460s, at an average speed of 185kmh, to win the San Marino Grand Prix. He won because, as we have seen, Patrese crashed.

On 2 May 1999, Michael Schumacher started third on the grid and covered 62 laps (305 kilometres) in 1h 33m 44.792s, at an average speed of 195kmh, to win the San Marino Grand Prix. He won because Häkkinen, leading comfortably, crashed on lap 18.

This, of course, was just a few days after Schumacher drove the 126 and Samson says that 'the very good thing is that just after having driven it Michael won at Imola, the first for Ferrari there for 17 years – Patrick, 1983. Again that must have told Michael what it meant. I saw him after and although I can't remember exactly what he said it was something like 'maybe it's been useful'. It seemed a bit strange, knowing him, to say something like that. I don't think he'd considered this part of the magic could happen: third on the grid just like Patrick, winning because Mika went off the track just like Patrese. . . .'

Tambay feels that the way it worked out was another of those strange things.

Final thoughts. The first from Tambay: 'I must say that today the car is in better shape than it was then. It was rebuilt before it was sold and it is maintained and run by the mechanics who were my mechanics then.'

The second from Samson. 'Patrick's birthday was near the time Schumacher drove the 126 and I asked Ferrari to give me one of the brake discs that Michael used to win at Imola. Michael signed this and I gave it to him and he was crying once again.'

And a Fact of Life to finish. 'We tried with *F1 Racing* magazine to have Michael drive Ferraris from the '50s, '60s, '70s and '80s,' Samson says. 'He was OK for that. "I would be delighted to do it, no problem." It didn't happen because of sponsors.'

The moods of
Suzuka . . .
Above, body

shells waiting.
Below, bodies
celebrating.

Chapter Seven

POLE TO
POLE

In April 2001 Schumacher was asked[1] if his 'success had
been devalued' because he had won his World
Championships partnered by Jos Verstappen, JJ Lehto,
Johnny Herbert and Rubens Barrichello. The implication –
and meaning no disrespect to these good men – was that if
Schumacher had been partnered by a genuine number one
driver (as Prost had been, for example, by Lauda, then
Senna) everything might have been different.

Schumacher replied: 'People always try to put it in a way
that I make my team-mates slower than where they are in
reality, but I think that is a load of rubbish. Why would a
team be interested in slowing down another driver for his
team-mate? There is no point in that.'

There is point, of course – especially if the team is paying
the thick end of $25 million to the man they consider as the
deliverer of their dreams and the thin end of a lot less than
$25 million to the driver who will support him. Schumacher,
moreover, was in a stronger position than any contractual
arrangements stipulated. He did deliver. Others – di
Montezemolo, Todt, Brawn, Byrne, Stepney – were arranging
the methods and machinery of this delivery, and doing so in
the most pragmatic way.

Without Schumacher, it suddenly all moved at a slower
pace on the track and didn't lead to anywhere. Irvine
couldn't do it when Schumacher hurt himself in 1999, and
across 2000 and 2001 Barrichello won once. Everybody
knows the truth: a team gravitates to its own power source
and revolves around that.

*A ritual of celebrating Schumacher's 2001 championship was
enacted at Monza, however much the mood was wrong for that
after the terrorist outrages of 11 September.*

Until Barrichello arrived, Martin Brundle was the team-mate to stay closest to Schumacher on the track. This is Monaco 1992 (above). Schumacher talks to Symonds and Ross Brawn, on the extreme left, listens. (Right) The mutual respect between Schumacher and Brundle has lasted to this day. (Opposite) Senna wins Brazil in 1993, Schumacher is a pensive third. Both men make themselves big. Senna's total of 65 pole positions seemed to be safe for generations but Schumacher could get past it.

Everyone knows, too, that the only proper comparison for a driver is his team-mate because (in theory and mostly in practice) they have the same cars. Across Schumacher's decade of Grand Prix racing he has had nine partners and, of 161 qualifying sessions, they managed to out-qualify him *only nine times*. This compares, incidentally, with Senna's total of 18 times, also from 161 qualifying sessions. We saw in Chapter 2 how disappointed he was not to outqualify Piquet when he made his début at Spa in 1991. The race after that, Monza, he joined Benetton and did partner Piquet. He outqualified him with 1:22.471 against Piquet's 1:22.726.

Here are the nine times Schumacher was outqualified. I give the pole time purely for context.

Australia (Adelaide), 1991. He had not, of course, driven Adelaide before: this was only his sixth Grand Prix, one less than the number of times team-mate Piquet had raced there. Here are their respective positions each session:

	1st practice	1st qual	2nd practice	2nd qual
Schumacher	11	5	5	5
Piquet	9	8	4	4

In that second qualifying, on a warm and overcast afternoon, Schumacher set his best time (1m 15.508) on the second of his two runs and so did Piquet (1m 15.291). From the Friday morning practice, Schumacher went progressively quicker as he became familiar with the track (1m 17.59/1m 15.44 on this Friday) but missed a gear on his fast lap in second qualifying. Schumacher would not be outqualified by a team-mate again for four years. It finished Piquet fifth (1:15.29) and Schumacher sixth (1:15.50). Pole: Senna, McLaren (1:14.04s).

Belgium (Spa), 1995. On the Friday all seemed well, Schumacher second to Berger's Ferrari (2:14.96 against 2:14.74). In the Saturday morning untimed session, however, he crashed and the car needed repairs before second qualifying. He managed ninth quickest on his first run (it

Brothers in arms. Schumacher with Riccardo Patrese (extreme left) who he outqualified 16 times out of 16. He outqualified Jos Verstappen (left, above) eight times out of eight. (Left) the shifting currrents of a qualifying session, to three decimal places. The 1997 Luxembourg Grand Prix (above) when he and Ralf kept the crash at the start in the family. Schumacher with Eddie Irvine (right) who he outqualified 55–4.

had been raining), Herbert fourth. Positions shifted as the weather shifted and Schumacher made another run, this one late. Twice the gearbox electronics changed down from sixth to fifth, ramming the Renault engine up to more than 19,000 rpm, which it couldn't take. He qualified sixteenth (1:59.07), Herbert fourth (1:56.08). Pole: Berger, Ferrari (1:54.39).

Australia (Melbourne), 1996. Only one qualifying session from now on, incidentally. Schumacher's first race for Ferrari, and Eddie Irvine's too. On the Friday Schumacher qualified fourth and Irvine seventh: Irvine had had oversteer and understeer the day before (Melbourne was a new circuit, the Thursday an introduction to it) and this still didn't feel right on the Friday. It did on the Saturday and Irvine thrust in 1:32.88. Schumacher was in the spare car because the gearbox had cracked in the morning and now he had a problem with the rear wing. He sensed he could not depose the Williamses of Villeneuve and Hill on the front row but thought he might get past Irvine's 1:32.88. He did a 1:33.12s, which was 0.24 of a second too slow. Irvine qualified third, Schumacher fourth. Pole: Villeneuve, Williams (1:32.37).

Austria (A1-ring), 1997. Irvine finished ahead of Schumacher although the difference was just about as close to nothing as you can reasonably get. The cars understeered, a major disadvantage at such a track. Ferrari put Irvine on soft tyres in a supreme effort to conjure a fast lap for him while Schumacher stayed on the hard Goodyear compound. He might have beaten Irvine even then but began to run out of fuel on what was potentially his hottest lap. That caused a small misfire. Irvine was eighth (1:11.051), Schumacher ninth (1:11.056). Pole: Villeneuve, Williams (1:10.30).

Germany (Hockenheim), 1998. Schumacher was decisively outqualified by Irvine this time, Irvine on the third row, Schumacher on the fifth – 'it is definitely the wrong time and the wrong place to have my worst qualifying of the season,' Schumacher said. He managed fifth after two runs but fell back as others improved. Irvine described the day as 'difficult' and a 'struggle'. Irvine qualified sixth (1:43.27), Schumacher ninth (1:43.45). Pole: Häkkinen, McLaren (1:41.83).

Spain (Barcelona), 1999. Irvine qualified on the front row, Schumacher on the second. This seemed mysterious, and Schumacher compounded that when he said that 'for reasons we must now investigate' it hadn't been as good in the afternoon as it had in the morning. This proved to be a small engine problem. Irvine finished second (1:22.21), Schumacher fourth (1:22.27). Pole: Häkkinen, McLaren (1:22.08).

Britain (Silverstone), 2000. New team-mate Barrichello took pole on a day of uncertain weather and made an early run 'because I thought it might rain later'. Schumacher changed the car's set-up for his last run. 'It did not pay off. On top of all that I made a couple of small mistakes which cost me precious time.' Pole: Barrichello (1:25.70), Schumacher fifth (1:26.16).

Austria (A1-ring), 2000. Barrichello outqualified Schumacher without extenuating circumstances. Schumacher put it bluntly: 'On my last run I had nothing to lose: I was fourth and I gave it my all. I went over my limit at Turn 4 and lost control of the car. I am quite a way off pole time, which worries me a little. Unlike our rivals, I have been unable to find the right balance between the slow and quick corners and that is very important on this track.' Barrichello insisted firmly that 'people have been saying the gap is getting bigger between Michael and me, but that's just not right.' Barrichello finished third (1:10.84), Schumacher fourth (1:11.04). Pole: Häkkinen (1:10.41).

Italy (Monza), 2001. Many thoughts were elsewhere because the meeting at Monza began three days after the 11 September terrorist attack on the United States. Schumacher, largely silent, reflected how sombre the whole mood was and admitted that he found concentration difficult. He pushed hard enough in qualifying but his runs did not look neat or controlled. Barrichello, meanwhile, found the right set-up. Barrichello finished second (1:22.52), Schumacher third (1:22.62). Pole: Montoya, Williams (1:22.21).

NOTE [1] Autosport.

From the beginning at Ferrari there was always a lot to think about – *sometimes in solitude with only your own shadow for company.*

Facts of the matter

When Barrichello took pole at Silverstone in 2000 it was the *only time* in Schumacher's career that a team-mate had ever done such a thing. The overview must be that if it was possible to force the car to take pole, Schumacher would do that – and Jos Verstappen, JJ Lehto, Johnny Herbert and Eddie Irvine, handling the same cars as he, could not. More than that, even when Schumacher had cars which couldn't get near pole he *still* forced the car to outqualify his team-mates except for these nine times.

Broadening this, I want to examine Schumacher's overall record against those pitted directly against him as his partner and, for interest, to do the same with Senna. Because they were in a sense contemporaries (between 1991 and 1994) it is possible to make a comparison in a way which is far more problematical with Fangio, Moss and Clark. This is what Schumacher and Senna did to those supposedly nearest and dearest to them. I have arranged the statistics (forgive me) like football scores in the Qualifying column, showing which driver 'won' in terms of out-qualifying the other.

Schumacher vs his team-mates

	Races	Qual	Poles	Wins		Races	Qual	Poles	Wins
1991 (Jordan)					**1996 (Ferrari)**				
Schumacher	1	1	0	0	Schumacher	16	15	4	3
De Cesaris	1	0	0	0	Irvine	16	1	0	0
1991 (Benetton)					**1997 (Ferrari)**				
Schumacher	5	4	0	0	Schumacher	17	16	3	5
Piquet	5	1	0	0	Irvine	17	1	0	0
1992 (Benetton)					**1998 (Ferrari)**				
Schumacher	16	16	0	1	Schumacher	16	15	3	6
Brundle	16	0	0	0	Irvine	16	1	0	0
1993 (Benetton)					**1999 (Ferrari)**				
Schumacher	16	16	0	1	Schumacher	10	9	3	2
Patrese	16	0	0	0	Irvine	10	1	0	2
1994 (Benetton)					**2000 (Ferrari)**				
Schumacher	8	8	2	5	Schumacher	17	15	9	9
Verstappen	8	0	0	0	Barrichello	17	2	1	1
Schumacher	4	4	3	3	**2001 (Ferrari)**				
Lehto	4	0	0	0	Schumacher	17	16	11	9
Schumacher	2	2	1	0	Barrichello	17	1	0	0
Herbert	2	0	0	0					
1995 (Benetton)					**TOTAL**				
Schumacher	16	15	4	9	Schumacher	161	152	43	53
Herbert	16	1	0	2	Team-mates	161	9	1	5

Senna vs his team-mates

1984 (Toleman)	Races	Qual	Poles	Wins
Senna	9	7	0	0
Cecotto	9	2	0	0
Senna	2	2	0	0
Johansson	2	0	0	0
1985 (Lotus)				
Senna	16	13	7	2
De Angelis	16	3	1	1
1986 (Lotus)				
Senna	16	16	8	2
Dumfries	15[1]	0	0	0
1987 (Lotus)				
Senna	16	16	1	2
Nakajima	16	0	0	0
1988 (McLaren)				
Senna	16	14	13	8
Prost	16	2	2	7
1989 (McLaren)				
Senna	16	14	13	6
Prost	16	2	2	4

[1] Dumfries did not qualify for Monaco

1990 (McLaren)	Races	Qual	Poles	Wins
Senna	16	12	10	6
Berger	16	4	2	0
1991 (McLaren)				
Senna	16	13	8	7
Berger	16	3	2	1
1992 (McLaren)				
Senna	16	15	1	3
Berger	16	1	0	2
1993 (McLaren)				
Senna	13	13	0	3
Andretti	13	0	0	0
Senna	3	2	1	2
Hakkinen	3	1	0	0
1994 (Williams)				
Senna	3	3	3	0
Hill	3	0	0	0
TOTAL				
Senna	161	143	65	41
Team-mates	161	18	9	15

Putting them together

	Races	Qual	Poles	Wins
Schumacher	161	152	42	53
Team-mates	161	9	1	5

	Races	Qual	Poles	Wins
Senna	161	143	65	41
Team-mates	161	18	9	15

That of all Schumacher's team-mates only one – Barrichello – took pole stands completely apart from Senna, and this may reflect that Senna had stronger team-mates, particularly Prost and Berger. Prost, however, accepted that in terms of absolute speed he could not match Senna and concentrated on racecraft, winning seven races in 1988 and four in 1989. (Interestingly, this was the same situation in 1984–85 when Lauda partnered Prost at McLaren. Lauda would remember 'I felt every bit as strong as Prost in the race proper, where I knew he didn't have the edge. The only thing was, I had to pay the penalty for poor qualifying times. To make up those places on the grid between Prost and myself, I had to take some additional risks in the race.' *To Hell and Back*, Verlag Orac, Vienna, *1985*). The point is that if Grand Prix racing was only about speed, every cowboy you meet at the traffic lights in a souped up Ford Escort would be World Champion, but they aren't.

Lauda was. Prost was. Schumacher is.

GREATEST OVERTAKING MOVE

Schumacher would say that beating Fangio's five World Championships 'is not really a target, and I don't think it would be a fair comparison anyway. What Fangio did in Formula 1 in his era was astounding. With cars going so fast and with so little safety, it appears to me exceptional, unbelievable. Without doubt I wouldn't have been able to do it. What we modern drivers do is pretty small in comparison. I've driven a fair few cars from the old days, and it is unbelievable the speeds they did.'

In 2000 Schumacher went past Senna's total of 41 wins but said 'the comparison is not honest. Ayrton was killed on the track and his record in Formula 1 would obviously have been completely different, today, without the accident.'

Prost took 193 races to win a record 51 victories, and Schumacher went past Prost in Belgium in 2001, his 158th race. All that, of course, means very little without a context, and the context has to be how strong the opposition was.

Prost's career ran concurrently with those of Piquet, Mansell and Senna himself and the quartet won 11 championships between them (not forgetting Keke Rosberg and Niki Lauda each winning one). Taking this as the yardstick, while Schumacher was winning his four championships Damon Hill managed one, Jacques Villeneuve one and Mika Häkkinen two.

Prost said at Hungary in 2001: 'When I retired at the end of 1993, I thought the first driver to reach my total would be Ayrton Senna. Alas he didn't have the time. Since then, the name Michael Schumacher imposed itself quite naturally. I

Laying rubber down as the parade lap begins at Silverstone in 1999.

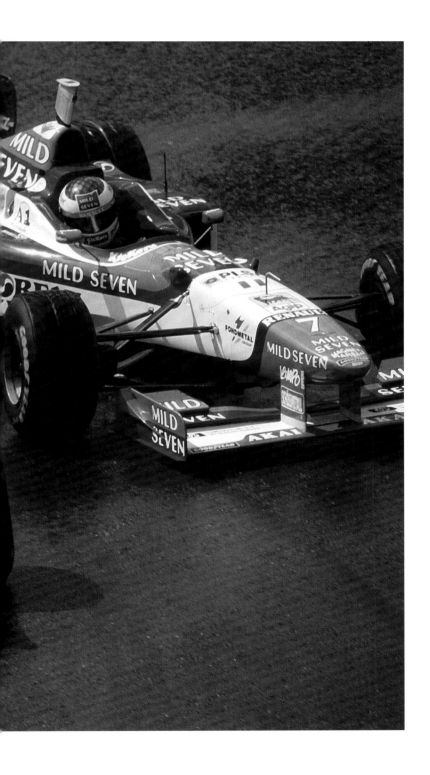

think his way of leading races is closer to that of Ayrton than to mine. At times he has behaved on the track in a way that I didn't but it's hard to make comparisons. The eras are different and the cars are not at all the same. In the turbo era, reliability was limited and to win three races in a season was often an achievement. Since then, with normally-aspirated engines, Formula 1 offers clearly superior reliability. In any case, Michael is an extraordinary chap and a formidable driver. I admire very much the way he has managed his career, and also the way he manages his own image.'

In an interview with Prost, Nigel Roebuck raised the matter of Schumacher constantly having a team-mate who had to defer to him, which Prost manifestly did not (John Watson in 1980, René Arnoux in 1981–82, Eddie Cheever in 1983, Lauda in 1984–85, Rosberg in 1986, Stefan Johansson in 1987, Senna in 1988–89, Mansell in 1990, Jean Alesi in 1991, Damon Hill in 1993).

Prost said 'if I'd had a team-mate just there to help me, I could have been World Champion two times more'. Prost stressed again the pitfalls of trying to compare Senna and Schumacher. 'I don't know how you can tell, because everything is so different now, the cars, the format of the races . . . it's impossible.'

So this chapter is not a comparison, or even an attempt at one (that will be coming later). This is simply Schumacher's progress to the record number of wins. Incidentally, Schumacher felt the best were Belgium 1992, Belgium 1995, Belgium 1996, Monza 1996, Monaco 1997, Budapest 1998, and Suzuka 2000.

That of these seven, three should be at Spa seems significant because as a circuit – and never forgetting the caprices of the weather – it is much closer to the traditional notion of racing than anywhere else. The significance of *that* is: however much Schumacher protests about the dangerous old days, the one circuit reflecting the old days, albeit distantly, is where he has been so dominant.

Belgium, 1997, and Schumacher overtakes Jean Alesi, running second – a decisive moment in victory number 26. On this same lap Schumacher overtook Villeneuve for a lead he would not lose.

The 52 wins . . .

Here they are, in sequence. It starts to get serious at win number 24 when he went past thrice World Champion Nelson Piquet's total. By number 28 he had Fangio, Lauda, Clark and Stewart behind him. Three drivers remained in the great overtaking panorama: Mansell on 31, Senna on 41 and Prost on 51 . . .

BELGIUM, 1992 (Benetton)

Second row. Spa offered its usual tantalising micro-climate. Schumacher pitted for wet tyres on lap four and worked his way from ninth place to third – then he went off and came back on behind his team-mate Martin Brundle. Schumacher noticed that Brundle's tyres were worn and 'immediately called the team' so that he could come in to change his own. He did – to slicks, the first of the front runners to do that. He led, and although Mansell in the Williams was catching him the exhaust on the Williams broke. *Podium: Schumacher 1h 36m 10.72s, Mansell @ 36.59s, Patrese (Williams) @ 43.89s.*

PORTUGAL, 1993 (Benetton)

Third row. He ran fifth to the first pit stops, then second behind Prost (Williams), and he decided not to make a second stop (for tyres – there was no refuelling in 1993). Prost pitted late – lap 29 – giving the lead to Schumacher. Prost hunted and harried him but couldn't get past. *Podium: Schumacher 1h 32m 46.30s, Prost @ 0.98s, Hill (Williams) @ 8.20s.*

BRAZIL, 1994 (Benetton)

Front row. Senna had pole and made a swift start, Alesi (Ferrari) nipping past Schumacher who needed a lap to re-take him. Schumacher led after the pit stops and cruised home once Senna, pursuing hard, spun off. By the end he had lapped the whole field. *Podium: Schumacher 1h 35m 38.75s, Hill @ 1 lap, Alesi @ 1 lap.*

PACIFIC, 1994 (Benetton)

Front row. Schumacher seized the lead from Senna (pole) who collided with Nicola Larini (Ferrari) at the first corner. Schumacher gave a crushing performance after that, so crushing that he didn't even lose the lead during his two pit stops. Again he lapped the whole field – except Berger (Ferrari). *Podium: Schumacher 1h 46m 01.69s, Berger @ 1m 15.30s, Barrichello (Jordan) @ 1 lap.*

SAN MARINO, 1994 (Benetton)

Front row. Senna dead, and a chilled, joyless victory in the wake of that. *Podium: Schumacher 1h 28m 28.64s, Nicola Larini (Ferrari) @ 54.94s, Häkkinen (McLaren) @ 1m 10.67s.*

MONACO, 1994 (Benetton)

Pole. Schumacher the reluctant inheritor of Senna's mantle: he drew the circuit of Monaco to him and laid his will across it, leading every lap. He led Berger by some 4 seconds after the opening lap (which made people reach back to Jim Clark for anything approaching this), made his first pit stop on lap 24 with enough time to keep the lead and did the same again at his second stop. *Podium: Schumacher 1h 49m 55.37s, Martin Brundle (McLaren) @ 37.27s, Berger @ 1m 16.82s.*

CANADA, 1994 (Benetton)

Pole. Schumacher had Alesi alongside and Berger behind. Schumacher – slow at the start – muscled the Ferraris and pulled away. He was making one stop and wasn't sure what the Ferraris were doing (Berger was to stop twice, Alesi once). Schumacher pulled further away and, when he felt absolutely secure, eased off, looking after the brakes and tyres. *Podium: Schumacher 1h 44m 31.88s, Hill (Williams) @ 39.66s, Alesi @ 1m 13.38s.*

FRANCE, 1994 (Benetton)

Second row. Schumacher made a tremendous start to lead but was harried by Hill (Williams). They both pitted on lap 21, Schumacher taking on less fuel than Hill. It was the pivotal moment, Schumacher due to stop three times and now drawing decisively away from Hill in a sustained sprint. Although Hill took the lead when Schumacher stopped again, Schumacher was now on fresh tyres and as Hill pitted a second time Schumacher vanished into the distance – emerging from the third stop he had 15 seconds over Hill and it was ample. *Podium: Schumacher 1h 38m 35.70s, Hill @ 12.64s, Berger @ 52.76s.*

HUNGARY, 1994 (Benetton)

Pole. Hill made a better start but Schumacher drove round the outside of him into the first corner and although Hill regained the lead when Schumacher made his first pit stop, the shape of the race was established: Schumacher on a three-stop strategy again, Hill on two, so that when Hill did stop Schumacher sailed by not to be caught again. *Podium: Schumacher 1h 48m 00.18s, Hill @ 20.82s, Jos Verstappen (Benetton) @1m 10.32s.*

EUROPE, 1994 (Benetton)

Pole. Hill took an immediate lead – but Schumacher was on three stops again. Hill led to the first of them but, after his own, found Schumacher ahead. Hill's refuelling rig had a problem and he couldn't take on as much fuel as he needed, forcing him to make his second stop early. Schumacher was gone towards victory by then. *Podium: Schumacher 1h 40m 26.68s, Hill @24.68s, Hakkinen @ 1m 09.64s.*

BRAZIL, 1995 (Benetton)

Front row. Schumacher led Hill as they completed lap 1 but Hill stayed with him. Schumacher pitted first and Hill used Schumacher's own tactic – a lung-bursting sprint – to build a margin, so that he retained the lead after his own pit stop. Hill, however, spun off when the car locked. Schumacher made his second stop of three, passing the lead to Coulthard, but caught up as Coulthard made his second stop. Schumacher sprinted himself and built a margin large enough to protect his third stop. *Podium: Schumacher 1h 38m 34.15s, Coulthard (Williams) @ 8.06s, Berger (Ferrari) @ 1 lap.*

SPAIN, 1995 (Benetton)

Pole. Schumacher powered into the lead, from Alesi, and held him at bay comfortably enough. Then he stretched the lead at around a second a lap – and he would only stop twice. Hill, moving up to second place when Alesi's engine failed, would stop three times. Superficially it seemed Hill might challenge him but the third stop proved too much. *Podium: Schumacher 1h 34m 20.50s, Herbert (Benetton) @ 51.98s, Berger (Ferrari) @ 1m 05.23s.*

MONACO, 1995 (Benetton)

Front row. Hill had pole but Schumacher claimed after the race that Benetton knew Hill would be stopping twice. They selected a single stop for themselves. Hill led but Schumacher, even carrying a heavier fuel load, was able to stay with him. When Hill made his first stop, on lap 23 of the 78, Schumacher was gone. *Podium: Schumacher 1h 53m 11.25s, Hill @ 34.81s, Berger @ 1m 11.44s.*

FRANCE, 1995 (Benetton)

Front row. Hill led, Schumacher behind. Benetton had a fluid pit stop strategy – two or three, as the race developed – and now Schumacher harried Hill. Schumacher pitted first and, emerging, found enough time to gain the lead when Hill pitted. Schumacher retained this through the second pit stops to the end. *Podium: Schumacher 1h 38m 28.42s, Hill @ 31.30s, Coulthard @ 1m 02.82s.*

GERMANY, 1995 (Benetton)

Front row. Hill led but, moving into the second lap, inexplicably went off at the first corner, presenting Schumacher with the race. Coulthard (Williams) struggled to stay with him and eventually fell away. It was all as simple as that. *Podium: Schumacher 1h 22m 56.04s, Coulthard @ 5.98s, Berger (Ferrari) @ 1m 08.09s.*

BELGIUM, 1995 (Benetton)

Eighth row. A chaotic build-up for Benetton, beset by Schumacher going off on the Saturday morning and the car having a gearbox problem. Wet qualifying produced a surreal grid, with Hill on the fourth row. From the eighth row Schumacher constructed a magnificent race. Completing lap 1 he was thirteenth, lap 2 tenth, lap 3 eighth, laps 4 and 5 seventh, laps 6 to 10 fifth, laps 11 to 13 fourth, lap 14 third (Hill now in the lead), lap 15 second – which became the lead as Hill pitted. A bewildering race too: at one point Schumacher circled on dry tyres in the wet. (It must also be said that, at moments, Schumacher kept Hill back very robustly indeed.) A late 10-second stop 'n' go penalty for Hill, for speeding in the pit lane, finally killed the race as a contest. *Podium: Schumacher 1h 36m 47.87s, Hill @ 19.49s, Brundle (Ligier) @ 24.99s.*

EUROPE, 1995 (Benetton)

Second row. Coulthard led from Schumacher – both on wet tyres – but Alesi (Ferrari) was on slicks and moved up from sixth. That produced a rush to the pits for slicks and gave Alesi the lead. Coulthard ran second but Schumacher overtook him. Schumacher caught Alesi although, on lap 52 of the 67, he had to make a third stop. The first had been essentially a tyre change, not much fuel put in. He emerged 24 seconds behind Alesi, with 16 laps left. Hill's Williams skated off the circuit, virtually giving the World Championship to Schumacher. He reasoned that he could attack with impunity, caught Alesi and – Alesi on worn tyres after only one stop – plundered the lead at the chicane, forcing Alesi to go wide or crash. *Podium: Schumacher 1h 39m 59.04s, Alesi @ 2.68s, Coulthard @ 35.38s.*

PACIFIC, 1995 (Benetton)

Second row. Schumacher confirmed the championship with deft Benetton strategy, which again they'd left fluid. Coulthard led in mid-race, Schumacher behind him, but Schumacher reversed that when Coulthard made his second stop. You know the rest: Schumacher at full bore and building enough of a margin to stop again and still win. *Podium: Schumacher 1h 48m 49.97s, Coulthard @ 14.29s, Hill @ 48.33s.*

JAPAN, 1995 (Benetton)

Pole. After drizzle everyone was on wet weather tyres. Schumacher led from Alesi and pulled away but Alesi drew up, only to be punished with a 10-second stop 'n' go penalty for jumping the start. That was lap 5 and two laps later Alesi was in again, for slicks. Schumacher was in for slicks himself on lap 10 while Alesi scythed up to second place. They duelled until the Ferrari's driveshaft failed and Schumacher ran smoothly home. *Podium: Schumacher 1h 36m 52.93s, Häkkinen @ 18.33s, Herbert @ 1m 23.80s.*

SPAIN, 1996 (Ferrari)

Second row. Schumacher's first masterpiece of movement at Ferrari (it was his seventh race for them). In abominably wet conditions he made a faltering start, hampered by a clutch problem, and could see so little that he didn't know what position he was in or even how many cars he overtook on the first lap. It was probably three or four. He finished that lap sixth and now Irvine in the other Ferrari spun (fifth), then Hill made a mistake (fourth). He overtook Berger in the Benetton (third), on lap 9 overtook Alesi in the other Benetton (second) and three laps later sailed past Villeneuve into the lead. He was driving at a different level from all the others, his sensitivity creating certainty where ten others crashed or spun off. *Podium: Schumacher 1h 59m 49.30s, Alesi @ 45.30, Villeneuve (Williams) @ 48.38s.*

BELGIUM, 1996 (Ferrari)

Second row. Schumacher's second masterpiece of movement, pressing the art of the possible to its limit. Villeneuve was fast away but Schumacher beat Hill into *La Source*. He set off after Villeneuve but couldn't catch him. The pace car was out at lap 13 (Verstappen's Footwork had crashed) and Schumacher pitted almost immediately, Villeneuve not for another two laps because of confusion in the Williams pit. Schumacher was feeling 'a lot of play' on the steering wheel – he'd been riding the kerbs hard to stay with Villeneuve at the start – and now stayed away from the kerbs. He made a second stop. Villeneuve emerged from his second stop fractionally ahead but Schumacher powered by into *Eau Rouge*. *Podium: Schumacher 1h 28m 15.12s, Villeneuve @ 5.60s, Häkkinen @ 15.71s.*

ITALY, 1996 (Ferrari)

Second row. As the race settled, Alesi led from Schumacher. Alesi made his only pit stop on lap 31 but Schumacher stayed out another couple of laps: long enough for him to travel at a searing pace and emerge from his own stop in the lead. He made only one mistake – a lapse of concentration, he'd admit – when he clipped the tyre markers at the chicane [the tyres were to stop the drivers riding the full width of the kerbing]. Schumacher clipped them so hard that the steering wheel was plucked from his hands. He re-gathered the Ferrari smoothly enough. *Podium: Schumacher 1h 17m 43.63s, Alesi @ 18.26s, Häkkinen @ 1m 06.63s.*

MONACO, 1997 (Ferrari)

Front row. Drizzle before the race, rain on the parade lap – and Schumacher had risked choosing the 'intermediate' Ferrari rather than the one set up for the dry. The Williamses were on slicks and so was Häkkinen. Schumacher simply drove away from them, with Giancarlo Fisichella (Jordan) in second place but falling away every lap. Barrichello (Stewart) took over second place and circled in the distance while, on lap 53, Schumacher went up the escape road at *Ste Devote* but very deliberately rotated the Ferrari and returned, effortlessly. ***Podium: Schumacher 2h 00m 05.65s, Barrichello @ 53.30s, Irvine @ 1m 22.10s.***

CANADA, 1997 (Ferrari)

Pole. Schumacher led but at his first pit stop gave that to Coulthard (McLaren) who, it seemed, would win; but the pace car was out after Olivier Panis (Prost) crashed and Coulthard, making a final stop, found that the McLaren stalled. He came back out but the race finished under the pace car so he could do nothing but follow it. ***Podium: Schumacher 1h 17m 40.64s, Alesi @ 2.56s, Fisichella @ 3.21s.***

FRANCE, 1997 (Ferrari)

Pole. Schumacher led from Frentzen (Williams) and it became a procession until, on lap 60 of the 72, heavy rain fell. On lap 63 Schumacher, holding an enormous lead, went off but recovered and continued *on slick tyres* to the end. ***Podium: Schumacher 1h 38m 50.49s, Frentzen @ 23.53s, Irvine @ 1m 14.80s.***

BELGIUM, 1997 (Ferrari)

Second row. The race started under the pace car because the track was wet. As at Monaco, Schumacher selected the 'intermediate' Ferrari. The pace car pulled off and, completing lap 4, Villeneuve led from Alesi and Schumacher. At *La Source* he went inside Alesi and at Rivage, the right-loop out in the country, he surged past Villeneuve. The race was decided. ***Podium: Schumacher 1h 33m 46.71s, Fisichella @ 26.75s, Frentzen @ 32.14s.***

JAPAN, 1997 (Ferrari)

Front row. Ferrari hatched a plan because Villeneuve had been banned from the race (failing to slow under a warning flag in Saturday free practice) but reinstated under appeal. Villeneuve, anticipating that he'd lose the appeal and forfeit any points he got in the race, aimed to hold Schumacher back: they were locked into a struggle for the World Championship. Villeneuve led, Schumacher let Irvine by – but made sure Häkkinen couldn't follow – and Irvine took Villeneuve. A complex race, Schumacher getting ahead of Villeneuve at the first pit stops and Irvine backed off to let Schumacher by, then making sure Villeneuve couldn't follow. ***Podium: Schumacher 1h 29m 48.44s, Frentzen @ 1.37s, Irvine @ 26.38s.***

ARGENTINA, 1998 (Ferrari)

28

Front row. Coulthard, pole, led but Schumacher elbowed through on lap 5: the cars touched. Schumacher was able to continue at full speed and the race turned on whether he could gain enough time to stop twice – Häkkinen was only stopping once. Schumacher could, and did. *Podium: Schumacher 1h 48m 36.17s, Häkkinen @ 22.89s, Irvine @ 57.74s.*

CANADA, 1998 (Ferrari)

29

Second row. Coulthard led from Schumacher to lap 19, when the McLaren's throttle linkage failed. Schumacher pitted and, emerging, seemed not to notice Frentzen coming up at him – Frentzen went off. Schumacher had to serve a 10-second stop 'n' go penalty for that. Fisichella led but both he and Schumacher had to make pit stops. When Fisichella stopped Schumacher stayed out another five laps, plundering fastest laps to protect his own stops. *Podium: Schumacher 1h 40m 57.35s, Fisichella @ 16.66s, Irvine @ 1m 00.05s.*

FRANCE, 1998 (Ferrari)

30

Front row. Schumacher made an extraordinary start, consolidated that and ran to the end for, perhaps, the most straightforward victory of his career so far. *Podium: Schumacher 1h 34m 45.02s, Irvine @ 19.57s, Häkkinen @ 19.74s.*

BRITAIN, 1998 (Ferrari)

31

Front row. The bizarre, surreal race: on lap 43 Schumacher, running second, lapped the Benetton of Alexander Wurz under a yellow flag – the track was awash. The stewards waited for 28 minutes – three minutes longer than the time limit for notification – before telling Ferrari that Schumacher would be given a 10-second penalty. There was also confusion over the application of the rules. Häkkinen slithered off and, as a precaution, Ferrari brought Schumacher in for the penalty on the final lap. It meant Schumacher crossed the line on the pit lane and won the race stationary. In fact the 10-second penalty was rescinded. *Podium: Schumacher 1h 47m 12.45s, Häkkinen @ 12.46s, Irvine @ 19.19s.*

HUNGARY, 1998 (Ferrari)

32

Second row. The race was decided by something approaching sleight of hand. Häkkinen led from Coulthard, Schumacher third. After the first pit stops Schumacher ran fourth behind Villeneuve and the team decided to move to a three-stop strategy. Villeneuve pitted, Schumacher sprinted and made his second stop – only 6.8 seconds. That and the sprint enabled him to lead after the McLarens had pitted. Ross Brawn told him he had to build a lead of 25 seconds in 19 laps to protect his third stop. Schumacher sprinted again and led by 29 seconds when he did stop. It was enough. *Podium: Schumacher 1h 45m 25.55s, Coulthard @ 9.43s, Villeneuve @ 44.44s.*

ITALY, 1998 (Ferrari)

Pole. Schumacher made a poor start and reached the first chicane fifth. He took Villeneuve to be fourth and, when Irvine had let him through, tracked the McLarens of Häkkinen and Coulthard but couldn't immediately get near them. When Coulthard's engine failed on lap 17, Schumacher took Häkkinen, who had handling problems anyway. *Podium: Schumacher 1h 17m 09.67s, Irvine at 37.97s, Ralf Schumacher (Jordan) @ 41.15s.*

SAN MARINO, 1999 (Ferrari)

Second row. Häkkinen led from Coulthard, Schumacher third, but at the end of lap 17 Häkkinen rode a kerb and the McLaren snapped into the wall. Schumacher realised he couldn't catch Coulthard and Ferrari moved to a two-stop strategy (Coulthard was on one). It meant Schumacher sprinted, closed up, pitted and had three clear laps to gain time before Coulthard pitted. He did, and held a five-second lead after his second stop. *Podium: Schumacher 1h 33m 44.79s, Coulthard @ 4.26s, Barrichello @ 1 lap.*

MONACO, 1999 (Ferrari)

Front row. Schumacher made a tremendous start, beating Häkkinen, pole, to *Ste Devote* and building a lead from there. He had soon settled to a pace Häkkinen couldn't stay with and made his single pit stop in great safety, emerging still in the lead. *Podium: Schumacher 1h 49m 31.81s, Irvine at 30.47s, Häkkinen @ 37.48s.*

AUSTRALIA, 2000 (Ferrari)

Second row. An inherited win – or was it? The McLarens of Häkkinen and Coulthard filled the front row, Häkkinen led from Coulthard but Schumacher was able to stay with them without 'pushing'. Coulthard dropped out on lap 12 with an engine failure and Häkkinen dropped out on lap 19 with an engine failure too. Race over. *Podium: Schumacher 1h 34m 01.98s, Barrichello (Ferrari) @ 11.41s, Ralf Schumacher (Williams) @ 20.00s.*

BRAZIL, 2000 (Ferrari)

Second row. McLaren, filling the front row again, selected a one-stop strategy, Ferrari two. That meant Schumacher had to get ahead of the McLarens as soon as possible and pull away from them. Schumacher did that, beating Coulthard from the line and overtaking Häkkinen as they moved into lap 2. Schumacher made his first stop on lap 20 but emerged 6.7 seconds behind Häkkinen. The race hung in a fine balance but Häkkinen's engine failed. Yes: race over – again. *Podium: Schumacher 1h 31m 35.27s, Fisichella (Benetton) @ 39.89s, Frentzen (Jordan) @ 42.25s.*

SAN MARINO, 2000 (Ferrari)

38 Front row. Häkkinen led, Schumacher after him – and Häkkinen held him to the first pit stops at virtually the mid-point of the race. However Häkkinen made his second stop early and that gave Schumacher three laps to sprint before his own. The familiar story. Schumacher sprinted hard enough to pit and keep the lead. *Podium: Schumacher 1h 31m 39.77s, Häkkinen @ 1.16s, Coulthard @ 51.00s.*

EUROPE, 2000 (Ferrari)

39 Front row. Häkkinen made an astonishing start, touching the Ferrari (which irritated Schumacher) and they ran in that order, Coulthard third. Rain fell and Schumacher applied pressure, slicing past Häkkinen at the chicane and pulling away – but both needed wet tyres and pitted for them. Schumacher led and, with the weather getting worse, stroked the Ferrari to go faster and faster. He made his second stop and took on enough fuel to run to the end. Häkkinen, pitting ten laps later, hadn't created enough of a gap to do that and keep the lead. Häkkinen pressed hard but Schumacher's control was never seriously threatened. *Podium: Schumacher 1h 42m 00.30s, Häkkinen @ 13.82s, Coulthard @ 1 lap.*

CANADA, 2000 (Ferrari)

40 Pole. Schumacher led from Coulthard and these two pulled away but Coulthard's engine had stalled before the parade lap and restarting it took longer than the regulations, bringing a 10-second stop 'n' go. Coulthard served that, his chances essentially destroyed. The weather broke and Schumacher tip-toed home despite, at one point, going off. *Podium: Schumacher 1h 41m 12.31s, Barrichello @ 0.17s, Fisichella (Benetton) @ 15.36s.*

ITALY, 2000 (Ferrari)

41 Pole. The sad win. Schumacher was leading as the race began but a crash elsewhere cost the life of a marshal. The pace car was out for ten laps and when it was gone Schumacher constructed a big lead over Häkkinen. It was enough. Afterwards Schumacher cried because he'd won at Ferrari's spiritual home of Monza – and stopped Häkkinen's charge: Häkkinen had won the last two races. *Podium: Schumacher 1h 27m 31.63s, Häkkinen @ 3.81s, Ralf Schumacher @ 52.43s.*

USA, 2000 (Ferrari)

Pole. Coulthard inadvertently jumped the start and led, Schumacher behind and calculating that Coulthard would be getting a 10-second stop 'n' go but feeling that Coulthard was holding him back so team-mate Häkkinen could attack. Schumacher took Coulthard on the inside. It rained briefly. Schumacher stayed on wet tyres until lap 16 and emerged still 11 seconds ahead of Häkkinen. Although Häkkinen cut deep into that, the McLaren's engine let go. *Podium: Schumacher 1h 36m 30.88s, Barrichello @ 12.11s, Frentzen @ 17.36s.*

JAPAN, 2000 (Ferrari)

Pole. The World Championship decider and Häkkinen led away, Schumacher behind. They circled together but Häkkinen held the lead through the first pit stops. Towards the second stops it drizzled and Häkkinen was in on lap 37 giving Schumacher two clear laps to sprint. He did and was able to stop and emerge with a four second lead. It rained and Schumacher had to treat his dry tyres cautiously. Häkkinen wouldn't surrender but Schumacher, even easing back, could not be caught. Ferrari had their first World Champion since 1979. *Podium: Schumacher 1h 29m 53.43s, Häkkinen @ 1.83s, Coulthard @ 1m 09.91s.*

MALAYSIA, 2000 (Ferrari)

Pole. Schumacher and Häkkinen rolled before the lights but Häkkinen broke the beam and Schumacher did not. Häkkinen would have a 10-second stop 'n' go. He led from Coulthard, Schumacher third. Anticipating the penalty, Häkkinen let Coulthard through. Coulthard began to construct a lead but on lap 13 went briefly off and pitted earlier than he would have done: grass in the radiator. Schumacher went through and, although Coulthard challenged him late in the race, he couldn't get past. *Podium: Schumacher 1h 35m 54.23s, Coulthard @ 0.73s, Barrichello @ 18.44s.*

AUSTRALIA, 2001 (Ferrari)

Pole. Another sad win, a marshal killed by a wheel from Villeneuve's BAR. Schumacher led from Häkkinen, the pace car came out following the Villeneuve accident and when it had gone Schumacher accelerated away from Häkkinen hard. Not that that mattered. Häkkinen's suspension failed and Schumacher moved comfortably to the victory. *Podium: Schumacher 1h 38m 26.53s, Coulthard @ 01.72s, Barrichello @ 33.49s.*

MALAYSIA, 2001 (Ferrari)

Pole. Schumacher moved cleanly away from Barrichello but on lap 3 both went off – and came back on (Schumacher 11th) – in rain which a lap later increased heavily. The rush to the pits for wets began and, settling after that, Schumacher cut through the field and led on lap 16. From there the Ferraris ran safely home. *Podium: Schumacher 1h 47m 34.80s, Barrichello @ 23.66s, Coulthard @ 28.55s.*

SPAIN, 2001 (Ferrari)

Pole. The lucky one. In fact it was so lucky that Schumacher said he didn't care to win races like this. He led from Häkkinen and held that through the first pit stops, even increasing it a little. He made his second stop on lap 43, Häkkinen seven laps later and with enough time to retain the lead. More than that, Schumacher had a severe vibration and slowed. Häkkinen moved into the final lap some 40 seconds ahead – and the clutch exploded. *Podium: Schumacher 1h 31m 03.30s, Montoya (Williams) @ 40.74s, Villeneuve @ 49.63s.*

MONACO, 2001 (Ferrari)

Front row. Coulthard, pole, had a problem getting away on the parade lap and started from the back, leaving a clear path for Schumacher into *Ste Devote* and the wide blue yonder. He went there. Häkkinen, second, retired on lap 16 with a suspension problem and Schumacher moved inevitably to victory. It was, as he said himself, straightforward. *Podium: Schumacher 1h 47m 22.56s, Barrichello @ 00.43s, Irvine @ 30.69s.*

EUROPE, 2001 (Ferrari)

Pole. Ralf Schumacher pressed his brother hard in the opening stages after a muscular start between the two but had a 10-second stop 'n' go penalty for crossing the white line coming from the pits, and the race was over. *Podium: Schumacher 1h 29m 42.72s, Montoya @ 4.22s, Coulthard @ 24.99s.*

FRANCE, 2001 (Ferrari)

Front row. Ralf, pole, led while his brother fended off Coulthard and then laid the pressure on. Ralf had a slow first pit stop, costing the lead, and his Williams was difficult to drive. Big brother pulled away and only lost the lead to Montoya during the second stops, regaining it when Montoya pitted. *Podium: Schumacher 1h 33m 35.63s, Ralf Schumacher @ 10.40s, Barrichello @ 16.38s.*

HUNGARY, 2001 (Ferrari)

Pole. A consummate drive, during which he only lost the lead during his pit stops, gave Schumacher his fourth World Championship and equalled Prost's total of wins. Schumacher had looked invincible all weekend, and was. *Podium: Schumacher 1h 41m 49.67s, Barrichello @ 3.36s, Coulthard @ 3.94s.*

BELGIUM, 2001 (Ferrari)

Second row. Montoya, pole, stalled before the parade lap and started from the back. The race was stopped after Luciano Burti (Prost) crashed heavily on lap 4 and, moving into the formation lap for the re-start, Ralf's Williams was still being worked on – he'd start from the back. Schumacher's second row position had become pole by default and he led the race throughout to – finally – overtake Prost. *Podium: Schumacher 1h 08m 05.00s, Coulthard @ 10.10s, Fisichella @ 27.74s.*

Facts of the matter

In his decade of Grand Prix racing, Michael Schumacher has won 53 races. After Belgium and overtaking Prost's record, he won the final Grand Prix of 2001 in Japan. Against that, his nine team-mates have won five: Herbert 2, Irvine 2 and Barrichello 1. (Irvine won four for Ferrari in 1999, but two of them were when Schumacher was absent, recovering from a broken leg at Silverstone.)

Expanding on this, Herbert inherited both victories – in 1995 – because Schumacher and Damon Hill crashed when they were up front and it seems unlikely that Herbert would have won either if they hadn't. That reduces it to three.

When Irvine won in Australia in 1999 Schumacher had a technical problem and started from the back of the grid. He got as high as third before more mechanical problems slowed him.

When Irvine won in Malaysia that same year, Schumacher had returned after the leg injury to help him – Irvine – win the World Championship and twice during the race waited for Irvine to catch him up, and let him go through. That reduces it to one.

When Barrichello won in Germany in 2000 Schumacher was involved in a crash with Giancarlo Fisichella (Benetton) at the start. That reduces it to nil.

I show no disrespect to Herbert, Irvine or Barrichello

and I know that a large number of races are decided by mechanical reliability and crashes but you cannot escape this singular fact: no team-mate has ever beaten Schumacher in a straight fight, even once. You can of course argue that Ferrari would not have permitted Schumacher's team-mates to beat him. After all, they ordered Mika Salo, deputising in 1999 when Schumacher was injured, to slow down and let Irvine win the German Grand Prix. Against that, it seems that Schumacher's team-mates never got close enough to him to bring team orders into play.

To spice all this, Barrichello made a move to assert himself just before the 2002 season: 'I do my own job. I don't care what Michael does or aims to do. I wake up every day to enjoy life and be a winner. I know Michael has built the team around himself and he is unbelievably good in the car but, the day I think my time to win is past I will stop.'

Barrichello pointed out that of all the team-mates Schumacher has had, he had got closest. It was true but it did not address the central question. If Ferrari felt that Barrichello was impeding Schumacher, and if both had a chance in the championship, would they just let them race? I wonder what, deep down, Barrichello felt the true answer was. Team orders are as old as the World Championship – and if drivers don't like them, tough.

THE BIGGEST QUESTION

A life, a career and history itself were compressed into a few seconds one June afternoon in 1979 and, when it was done, Juan-Manuel Fangio signed autographs as if nothing had happened at all.

He'd been driving a Mercedes W125, a pre-War racing car of brutish power, at Donington Park. 'Experiments with higher alcohol content fuels gave a power output of 646bhp at 5800rpm,' wrote Cyril Posthumus. 'Some idea of the enormous potentiality of this new power unit can be gained from the fact that it developed 248bhp at a mere 2000rpm.'[1]

'The designers had developed a machine whose performance would not be surpassed for decades, indeed until 1965. It could be driven at 120kmh [74mph] in first gear, 185 [114] in second, 215 [133] in third and 270 [167] in fourth gear. It could, with special gear ratios, achieve 300kmh [186] and, with aerodynamically developed streamlined bodywork used for record attempts and for racing at Avus [the ultra-fast Berlin circuit] was capable of 400kmh [248].'[2]

Fangio was being presented with a monster.

He had never seen the car or Donington before and hadn't driven in a Grand Prix for two decades. He was aged 68. He wasn't, now, racing the Mercedes but giving a demonstration run[3] and thereby hangs a tale – because, rounding the corner onto the pit lane straight, he fed in too much of that brutish power and hung the tail out, a long way out. He caught that instantaneously. It happened so fast that Nigel Roebuck, covering the event, had barely registered

Schumacher rides the storm in Barcelona, 1996, winning his first race for Ferrari and destroying all opposition. He beat Alesi by 45 seconds, Villeneuve by 48 – and nobody else was even on the same lap when it finished.

that Fangio was in trouble when Fangio had got himself out of trouble 'with almost casual ease'.

Roebuck wrote: 'The next few minutes were unforgettable. As he grew accustomed to car and circuit, Fangio went faster and faster, the slides out of the chicane now anticipated and clearly relished. In the pits, Dan Gurney [an American veteran] like the rest of us was almost unable to believe his eyes, whooping and cheering and clapping his hands. There was spontaneous applause every time around, and on one occasion, after a particularly majestic power slide, Fangio acknowledged it with a bow of his head as he crossed the finish line.'[4]

Fangio won five World Championships between 1951 and 1957, and 24 of the 51 Grands Prix he contested. It remains a staggering strike rate even after all these years.

(As an aside, David Coulthard drove a 1937 W125 at the Mercedes test track at their Stuttgart headquarters in 1997. He was constricted from seeing what the car would really do for reasons of its antiquity and value. In spite of that he made it go fast enough to realise how inadequate by modern standards the brakes were, and was visibly shaken by that when he stopped. He expressed incomprehension that such a car could have been taken round the old Spa circuit at high speed. I include Coulthard's observations because they are interesting in themselves, but more interesting in the light of what Fangio did.)

Barcelona in that storm, and Schumacher cuts cleanly past Villeneuve for the lead.

The biggest question, as Michael Schumacher took his fourth championship in 2001, was twofold: would he go on to equal and then beat Fangio's five titles, and where would his place in history be? With Fangio? With Moss, Clark and Senna, who have long been included whenever the biggest question is asked so that now we truly do have The Famous Five? There is, of course, no unanimity about even this, never mind whether the question can actually be answered. Jo Ramirez – who worked in Grand Prix racing from 1962, latterly as team co-ordinator at McLaren until his retirement at the end of 2001 – says 'for sure I agree with Fangio, Schumacher, Senna, Clark . . . but I'd rather put Stewart and Alain Prost before Moss. Moss could drive

anything and he was brilliant and I liked him enormously but purely in terms of Grand Prix racing I don't think you could put him in front of Alain.'

The reason I put Moss in is that – however intangible, however vague – there is a groundswell of opinion down all these years that he must be in. His brilliance, his car command, his speed, his ability to bring a race to life cannot be doubted. Prost, the technocrat, did not do that. Prost was a minimalist, Moss a life-enhancer.

Younger readers, who have grown up with Schumacher will have heard talk of these great drivers without, perhaps, knowing quite who they were and what they did. Here they are.

CURRICULUM VITAE. Jean-Manuel Fangio, born 24 June 1911, Balcarce, Argentina. **He was from a poor family but managed to buy a Model T Ford and raced it. He became so outstanding that he needed the world stage. He first visited Europe in 1948 and drove in Grands Prix from 1950 to 1958 with, as a centrepiece, a victory at the Nürburgring in 1957 after a pit stop went wrong and he had to regain some 50 seconds. He was known as a sportsman and a gentleman. He is the yardstick by which all drivers are measured because he exercised an imperious command of the races. Grand Prix career 1950–1958.**

It is, however, a measure of Moss that he finished second in the World Championship in 1955, 1956, 1957 and 1958 and, across the first three of those years, he was beaten by Fangio but was arguably the only man who could push him, certainly on anything approaching a regular basis.

CURRICULUM VITAE. **Stirling Moss, born 17 September 1929, London. While accepting that Fangio was a better Grand Prix driver, Moss takes absolute consolation from the knowledge that he was a better sports car driver. Moss prides himself on his 'versatility' – books have been written detailing all the cars he raced. He became synonymous with speed in Britain, and speeding motorists were habitually asked by the traffic police 'who do you think you are, Stirling Moss?' He, too, was a sportsman and a gentleman. Grand Prix career 1951–1961.**

I suspected that, from the start of a Grand Prix to the first corner, Moss would cede to no man except Fangio. He said 'it's easier to follow than to lead. Anyway I was quite content to sit behind him to see the way the master did it!' However if they had been in sports cars, 'no way' would Fangio have beaten him. 'That wouldn't have come into the equation.'

CURRICULUM VITAE. **Jim Clark, born 4 March 1936, Kilmany, Fifeshire, Scotland. He had an ability so deft and delicate that quantifying it remains elusive. A modest man, he had no idea what it really was. As engine designer Brian Hart says, teams looked at their stop-watches not to know how fast their driver had gone but how far behind Clark he was. Clark only ever drove for Lotus in Formula 1 and his partnership with Colin Chapman, designer genius as well as owner of the team, remains a cornerstone of motor racing history. Grand Prix career 1960–1968.**

He and Moss competed against each other in Formula 1 in 1961, Moss's final season.

Senna was always profoundly interested in Clark's career and once, discreetly, went to the museum in Duns, on the Scottish borders, which is dedicated to Clark. He asked the curator what manner of man Clark was – the assembled trophies were of secondary interest. He had plenty of his own.

CURRICULUM VITAE. **Ayrton Senna, born 21 March 1960, Sao Paulo, Brazil. He was consumed by the need to win and was *mentally* capable of taking a racing car to its ultimate. I once asked Ken Tyrrell who was the fastest of all the drivers he had seen – nothing to do with any aspect of driving except speed. 'Senna' he said with barely any hesitation. At moments, Senna seemed touched with grace, at others captive to a savage intensity. Grand Prix career 1984–1994.**

For the sake of consistency Schumacher is included here in the same format as the other four.

CURRICULUM VITAE. **Michael Schumacher, born 3 January 1969, Hürth-Hermülheim, Germany. His early career was good rather than outstanding but he developed carefully, especially with Mercedes in the World Sports Car Championship, to the point where the full range of his abilities could be demonstrated the moment he reached Formula 1. From then he grew to be monumental. Grand Prix career 1991–present.**

Of course drivers can't show their versatility these days, can they? Schumacher gets the Renault Clio almost onto two wheels at the Schumachers' kart track at Kerpen, near Cologne. Weber, who must have seen all this before, sits it out. The US Grand Prix 2001, and Schumacher says farewell to Jo Ramirez (right), a friend to the whole of Formula 1 for three decades and a backbone of the McLaren team.

Clearly there is no definitive answer to the Biggest Question, but it is legitimate – and perhaps necessary – to ask it, now that Schumacher is slaughtering all manner of records and will clearly slaughter plenty more. Records are a currency in themselves, but not necessarily *the* currency although when they are coming at you with the speed and scale of Schumacher's, you can no longer ignore them. Moreover, merely asking produces instructive (and sometimes provocative) responses.

Here are the words of Stirling Moss. 'Fangio, I suppose, had regularity. In other words, whatever he could do he could do continually. This is an interesting thing. Look at every Grand Prix when it's over: find what pole position had been and notice that the drivers never get to it in the race. In 1961 at Monaco I had pole and if I'd done every lap at that pole pace – the whole hundred laps – I'd only have been 40 seconds quicker than I was.[5] Now it is such a specialised thing. There are certain drivers out there who are fast but when the race is on they don't do it the same way as qualifying.

'Why I'm using that is to show that whatever Fangio could do, whatever it was, he could do it tomorrow, the day after and the day after that: all the time. Two, he didn't waste any effort. In going round a corner he was precise because he would very rarely ever hang the back out' – which makes the compression at Donington even more remarkable.

'The Goodwood Festival of Speed is very revealing. You have these guys who are amateurs and most of them come round and they are overdoing it. You never saw that with Fangio. He didn't waste any effort. These guys are wasting effort, they're wasting rubber. Fangio was a precise man and Formula 1 in those days, not now, required precision. A fast car at Monaco – look at any picture – would brush the tyres against the barriers. Now they have these chamfered curves and some go here and some go there. . . .'

Jackie Stewart, thrice World Champion, underlines this difference. 'You know, in my entire career I had 17 pole positions. In those days, of course, there were longer practices – sometimes three hours long – and you used those practices to set the car up. And as long as you were up front it was a question of being able to have a car that would race the distance – from a heavy fuel load to a light fuel load, no change of tyres. Ken Tyrrell and I, for example, really did work endlessly on what was the best full race performance car. So pole was nice to have but that was all.'

Schumacher and the Ferrari people also work endlessly on the best race performance and this is what happens when they find it: at the Hungaroring in August 1998, Häkkinen (McLaren) took pole with 1:16.973, Schumacher on the second row with 1:17.366. As the race unfolded, Schumacher found himself running third behind Häkkinen and Coulthard so Brawn decided to change the strategy from two pit stops to three. Famously he told Schumacher over the radio 'you have 19 laps to make up 25 seconds'. Schumacher drove those 19 laps in qualifying mode, although even he could not of course get near his 1:17.366. His best race lap was 1:19.286. With the modern car set up in such different ways for qualifying and race it was intrinsically impossible even for Schumacher to get nearer. What he did do, however, was force the Ferrari down into the 1:19s four times – laps 45, 46, 48 and 54 – and then as he approached the third pit stop he forced this:

Lap 58	1:19.625
Lap 59	1:19.966
Lap 60	1:19.286
Lap 61	1:19.510

Coulthard's best lap was 1:20.546 and Jacques Villeneuve, who finished the race third in the Williams, 1:20.078. Nobody but Schumacher did a lap of 1:19. When he pitted he had gained 26.6 seconds over Coulthard so that he even had a margin over Brawn's demand for 25 seconds. Brawn, one of the most experienced operators in Grand Prix racing, watched this stunned. He says that Schumacher 'doesn't seem to struggle to drive the car on the edge for as long as is necessary. It just doesn't seem to take much out of him mentally or physically.'

The timeless theme is that, in their circumstances, Fangio and Moss were faster than anybody else competing against them, so was Stewart, and Senna had so much speed in qualifying that it scattered a generation of opponents. Schumacher was not flamboyant about such matters but, at the Hungaroring, he proved beyond reasonable doubt that he could have run with them.

Nor is it simply a matter of drawing up a short list – The Famous Five – and relegating the rest to the second division. 'All I've ever said, and I sincerely believe it is the correct way to look at it, is this: all we *can* look at is who was the undisputed leader of the era in which that person lived,' Stewart says. 'Fangio was the undisputed leader however good Farina was or Ascari was. There was no doubt that Fangio was the regular winner. He moved teams and cars as he saw fit to match his talents. So if it was Ferrari or Maserati or Mercedes-Benz or whoever he drove for, he would flip-flop them all the time to get the best. Enzo Ferrari hated him because of that. Ferrari expected loyalty but he never gave loyalty back. If you go from Fangio, the next real leader was Jim Clark. That combination of Colin Chapman and Jim Clark was unbeatable and however good Graham Hill was or Jack Brabham or Dan Gurney and everybody else, at that time Jim Clark was the undisputed leader.

Schumacher's demonstration run at Silverstone 2001 in the 1961 Ferrari . . .

'Maybe I was that next one and then there was Niki, who dominated the mid-1970s, and then there was unquestionably Prost, and then Senna and now Schumacher.'

Broadening that, 'nobody knows if, say, Jean-Claude Killy's record of Olympic gold medals in the giant slalom, the slalom and the downhill will ever be done again because it is now a different build of man, a different race of man [in ski racing, where the events have their specialists].[6] So you would *only* look at the time when Michael Schumacher lived, and you'd say he was the best. To start trying to wave a wand and conjure magical visions and see Schumacher in a car and Fangio and Clark or anybody else with him is for nobody to judge because it can't be done.'

In the absolute sense, you cannot argue with this but I intend to push the idea further because it gets more intriguing.

Straight away we must confront a fundamental difference between yesterday and today. The versatility which Moss holds so dear, and which seems to argue the full range – and therefore quality – of a driver, is almost unavailable now. Moss says 'the rules stop that because the drivers have allowed the rules – or the organisers and team owners have made the rules – that you can't race more than one car in a day. They can't do a curtain-raiser in a touring car or a sports car. In my day you not only had all that lot, you had the Race of Champions[7] and we raced in that for nothing.

'I drove right across the board and I think it is a very important thing. I know from other people I meet, people of my era, that they enjoyed being able to race against the top Formula 1 drivers in saloon or sports cars. People say "I raced against you in some race somewhere" and I think that is part of it. And I was very lucky. My career was following the war when there weren't the established stars. I hadn't got to knock anybody down – unlike now when anybody coming in will have to knock Michael off the top. I was lucky I didn't have that.'

Silverstone . . . Schumacher seems to be saying 'I survived!'

Well, Moss had Fangio but never mind. . . .

Accepting that the modern driver cannot brandish a Curriculum Vitae anything like that of Moss, there *are* examples, however sparse and sometimes unsatisfactory, of this versatility. For example, the following Grand Prix drivers have won the Le Mans 24-hour sports car race since 1990: Martin Brundle, Bertrand Gachot, Johnny Herbert, Derek Warwick, Yannick Dalmas, Mark Blundell, Mauro Baldi, JJ Lehto, Alexander Wurz, Michele Alboreto, Stefan Johansson, Pierluigi Martini and Emanuele Pirro.

When Schumacher drove Le Mans with the Mercedes team in 1991 he was partnered by Karl Wendlinger and Fritz Kreutzpointner, making his sports car début, as we saw in Chapter 2. None had seen Le Mans before but Schumacher set fastest lap (3:35.564, an average of 141mph/226kph) which a contemporary report describes as 'stunning'. Wendlinger crashed the car and they finished fifth.

That season Schumacher drove in seven other rounds of the World Sports Car Championship, taking a second place at Silverstone and, partnered by Frentzen, winning Autopolis in Japan. Schumacher took the first stint, moving up from sixth on the grid and cutting inside Warwick to be third at Turn One. By lap nine he was with the leaders and took Teo Fabi (Jaguar) on the *outside* of Turn One. The leading car dropped out with oil pressure problems and Schumacher had the win. 'I'm really happy for myself, but more for the team. They have done such a big work this year it's unbelievable. To keep all the time the motivation to continue like this, it was really hard.'

Sound familiar?

As a curious historical footnote, Fangio, Moss and Clark competed at Le Mans but never won it. Senna, who never went there, did however compete in a round of the World Sports Car Championship with the Joest team at the Nürburgring in 1984. As a complete stranger to the team and the car he did a fast lap in the wet and then, reputedly, asked what all the dials on the dashboard meant! The car, a Porsche 956, had mechanical problems in the race although the team owner, Reinhold Joest, adored Senna overtaking another car on the outside – and was astonished when, after the race, Senna came to him with a long list of ways he felt the car could be improved.

Incidentally, Moss says that the difference between Formula 1 and sports cars is 'rather like writing with a very fine nib, which is Formula 1, or the broad nib, which is the sports car. It's much easier to make your writing look good with a broad nib. Moreover, Formula 1 was always where the line between right and wrong was very, very fine.' Surveying it, there can be no doubt that these great ones could write both ways, and virtually at will.

In May 1984 Senna competed in a race of Mercedes 190Es – the saloon car – to inaugurate the new Nürburgring. The celebrity entry included Lauda, Rosberg, John Watson, Denny Hulme, Scheckter, James Hunt, Jack Brabham, John Surtees and Moss. The drivers regarded it as fun, all except for Senna who, Watson believes, saw it as a chance to advance his career by winning, and did win (from Lauda). Senna once spent a day in mid-Wales driving a variety of rally cars on the equivalent of a special stage and,

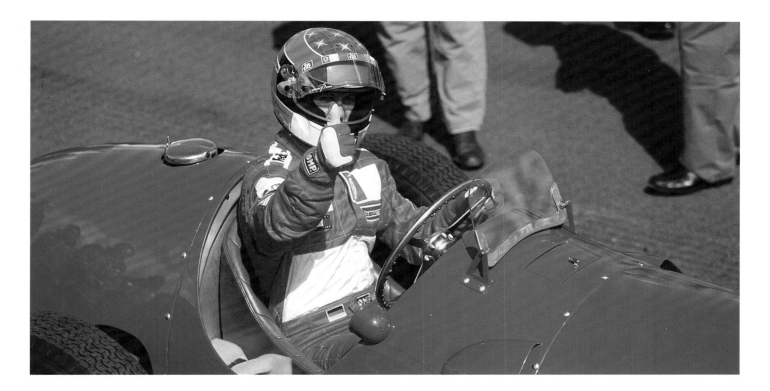

by close of play, had adapted to the point where he was making them go fast.

There is no comparison between this, of course, and what Jim Clark did, entering the RAC Rally, taking Lotus Cortinas round Brands Hatch, mostly on two wheels, and winning Indianapolis.

Historian Doug Nye suggests that Clark, who he met, was 'curious to know' what various sorts of cars would do and, when he had found out, his curiosity was satisfied. This may have been why he accepted an invitation to drive a 1936 ERA racing car during the French Grand Prix meeting at Rouen in 1962.

Gregor Grant in *Autosport* wrote: 'Jim Clark was persuaded to try Patrick Lindsey's ERA He turned in three laps, and shook everyone by getting down to 2 mins 48.7 secs, a really splendid time for such a veteran machine.' Nye says Clark hardly used the brakes, simply slaloming through the corners.

Pole for the Grand Prix was taken by Clark in the Lotus at 2m 9.6s, so that – over the 4.06 mile course – he was not absurdly slower in the pre-War sit-up-and-beg car!

In the Golden Age Motor Race at the meeting (10 laps) Lindsey won in the ERA and set a fastest lap of 2m 50s – more than two seconds slower than Clark, who of course had never driven the car before. (Nye points out, however, that Clark's time was set after qualifying, the Golden Age was on race day when the weather was very different *and* there was oil on the track. This does not in any way diminish Nye's regard for Clark – a 'genius', and he uses that word for Schumacher as well. 'What they have is what 99.99% of the rest of the world does not have. What is it? Well, whatever it is it defies rational analysis.')

Jim Endruweit was a Lotus mechanic at Rouen. 'We were not unnaturally fairly busy with our own business getting ready for the Grand Prix. The owner of the ERA contacted Jimmy – came to see him or whatever – with the outcome that Jimmy was going to drive this car. I probably didn't even know it was an ERA! Jimmy drove it and the owner was standing there sweating a bit. Jimmy bimbled by – drove past looking very relaxed – on his first lap, and he was quick, next lap he was quicker. He did a time that the owner thought was out of this world, couldn't believe. Jimmy brought it in and the car was fine, it wasn't even sweating. It seemed remarkable that he could get into – or onto – such a vehicle and drive it amazingly quickly without flogging it. How did Jimmy take that? As far as I know, he didn't think he had done anything remarkable. "Yeah, that was fine, I enjoyed that." He was tremendously relaxed about that sort of stuff.'

I asked Jo Ramirez why Clark was so much better than others of his era? 'Like Schumacher and Senna, they are just born with it. They didn't have to work hard at it at all. I regret about modern Grand Prix racing that you don't see the drivers driving anything else. One of the greatest things was watching Jim Clark in the Lotus Cortina round Brands on two wheels and lapping a second and a half quicker than anybody else. He'd have the nearside wheel above the grass and the other wheel just touching the apex of the corner, and the car just about to roll. You'd think *he will roll, he must roll* – but he didn't. He was idolised by all the other drivers.' Ramirez adds a tantalising postscript. Those same drivers thought 'if Clark could do it, it can be done'. Not by them though.

Jackie Stewart concedes that the great ones have always been versatile 'but that changed and is no longer the case. For example, one or two of the guys go and drive a touring car against the top drivers there – say in Germany – it's always tough for them to dominate in that. Some people in the old days could. I remember winning four races on the same day at Crystal Palace in four different racing cars – you might go from a Formula 3 car to a Lotus Elan to an E-Type Jaguar.

'In Michael's case that hasn't shown up for a while. Since he left sports cars with Mercedes you haven't seen him apart from one or two karting events, and he drove at Silverstone. What I'm saying is that today the specialist

One test of true greatness is how drivers exploit treacherous conditions when those around them can't. In Spain in 1992 Schumacher, still inexperienced, pushed Nigel Mansell hard. . . .

lives, the generalist is no longer there. That makes it a very narrow band that these guys work in.'

We've already seen how Schumacher handled Tambay's 1983 turbo Ferrari and how, like a very modern man, his thoughts were dominated by safety – a precise reflection of the world he grew up in and no reflection on his ability. At Silverstone in 2001, he took part in a commemoration of Ferrari's first Grand Prix victory – there – on 14 July 1951. An engineer who worked on the car that day, Ener Vecchi, was present to see Schumacher take the car (which evidently he'd said would need work done on its brakes!) for a demonstration run. The car was described as the 'sister' of the one Froilan Gonzalez won in. Schumacher said 'to drive it is an absolute pleasure' and he made it go a bit on the straights.

No doubt any competent driver could have done the same. The point I'm trying to establish is much broader: however fragmentary the evidence, it implies that Senna and Schumacher would have been formidable driving the wide variety of cars which Clark, Moss and Fangio did; that they were not just robotic specialists cushioned by technology. If you accept that then you can approach The Biggest Question now that The Famous Five are competing with equal equipment, as the saying goes.

NOTES

[1] *The Racing Car*, C. Clutton, C. Posthumus and D. Jenkinson (Batsford, 1962)

[2] *The Complete History of Grand Prix Motor Racing*, Adriano Cimarosti (Aurum, 1997).

[3] As part of the Gunnar Nilsson Memorial Trophy Race Meeting.

[4] *Autosport*, 7 June 1979.

[5] In 1961, Moss took pole at Monaco with a lap of 1:39.1 and by mid-point in the race was below that (1:38.6) before he set joint fastest lap at 1:36.3 on lap 85.

[6] At the Winter Olympics in Grenoble, 1968, Killy won the downhill, the slalom and the giant slalom. Then the specialists came. Even four years later, at Sapporo, different ski-racers won each of the three events.

[7] A non-Championship Formula 1 race run from 1965 to 1983 at Brands Hatch.

Facts of the matter

A measure of a driver's capabilities is how he performs in wet races, because the most delicate car control and sensitivity are needed. Here are the wet races of The Five. They are not intended to be comparative because, by definition, a race run on the old Spa – Belgian country roads, uneven cambers, trees, ditches, houses – in a car with narrow tyres during a thunderstorm was a different creature to one run on wide, wet-weather tyres round the new Spa during light rain. What these paragraphs *do* demonstrate is how good each of The Five was, and how few mistakes they made. Note how few crashes there are. I have not adhered to any strict definition of a wet race (one officially designated so) but, rather, included all races where it rained – even if that was a shower.

FANGIO: Switzerland 1951, first; Britain 1953, second; Argentina 1954, first; France 1954, first; Britain 1954, fourth; Holland 1955, first; Belgium, 1956, did not finish, transmission; Italy 1956, eighth.

MOSS: Switzerland 1951, eighth; Belgium 1952, engine failed on lap 1; Holland 1952, engine failed on lap 74 when seventh; Britain 1954, rear axle failed on lap 81 when second; Holland 1955, second; Belgium 1956, lost wheel; Italy 1956, first; Monaco 1960, first; Britain 1961, had been as high as second, brake pipe failed on lap 45; Germany 1961, first.

CLARK: Britain 1961, oil leak on lap 63 when fifth; Germany 1961, fourth; Germany 1962, fourth; Belgium 1963, first; France 1963, first; Belgium 1965, first; Belgium 1966, engine failed on lap 1; Britain 1966, fourth; Germany 1966, accident on lap 12; Canada 1967, ignition failed on lap 70 when leading.

SENNA: Monaco 1984, second; Portugal 1985, first; Belgium 1985, first; Britain 1988, first; Germany 1988, first; Japan 1988, first; Canada 1989, seventh; Belgium 1989, first; Australia 1989, crashed when leading; Canada 1990, first; Brazil 1991, first; San Marino 1991, first; Spain 1991, fifth; Australia 1991, first; Spain 1992, spun on lap 63 when third; Belgium 1992, fifth; Brazil 1993, first;

Steps through the storms. In Brazil in 1993 (above) he drove prudently to third place while cars spun off everywhere. This (above right) is his pit stop in that race: easy does it. Moving through standing water (right).

Europe 1993, first; San Marino 1993, hydraulics failure after 42 laps when second.

SCHUMACHER: Australia 1991, collision after 5 laps when fifth; Spain 1992, second; Belgium 1992, first; Brazil 1993, third; Europe 1993, crash on lap 23 when fifth; San Marino 1993, second; Canada 1994, first; Japan 1994, second; Belgium 1995, first; Europe 1995, first; Japan 1995, first; Brazil 1996, third; Monaco 1996, crashed on the first lap; Spain 1996, first; Belgium 1996, first; Monaco 1997, first; France 1997, first; Belgium 1997, first; Britain 1998, first; Belgium 1998, crash on lap 26 when leading; France 1999, fifth; Europe 2000, first; Canada 2000, first; Belgium 2000, second; Japan 2000, first; Malaysia 2001, first; Brazil 2001, second.

Jim Endruweit was at the Nürburgring with Clark and Lotus in 1962. 'It was a dreadful race, atrocious weather. Jimmy was on the front row and fluffed the start – I think his engine stalled – and he went off at the back of the field. He worked his way up – Dan Gurney, Graham Hill and John Surtees occupying the first three places – and caught them from being four *minutes* behind or whatever. When he reached fourth he stayed there. When

he came in we were talking about it and he said "well, I frightened myself a bit" and he backed off to the same speed as the leaders. He was almost in cruising mode as he did that, and on The Ring in that weather it was unbelievable. He normally didn't drive that fast. No matter what he was doing he virtually always had something in hand.' (The Nürburgring was 22.7km/14.1m but even so Clark overtook either 15 or 16 cars on the opening lap. On lap 11 of the 15, according to one account[1] 'the car went into a horribly long slide and counter-slide, and Clark decided to ease up.')

Certainly Stirling Moss feels that Schumacher is 'exceptionally good, yes, but so was Senna. The great ones all are, of course. You have to be. That's what makes some great and the others very good.'

When Senna won the European Grand Prix at Donington in 1993, his performance in changing weather conditions was so overwhelming – at one point he led by a whole lap – that Jo Ramirez could not believe it. 'Mega, absolutely mega. That was the race that showed the world how good he was, especially those first two laps.'

Could Schumacher have driven those two laps?

'I think no, but I'd also say I'm biased. He's immensely quick in the wet, but. . . .'

What is it that they have?

'They feel the car so much better than the rest and that

enables them to anticipate much better too. The only one of those great drivers who wasn't so good in the wet was Alain Prost. In Alain's mind was the visibility: in the wet it's very, very hard to see. He never forgot that he and one of his great mates, Didier Pironi, crashed at Hockenheim in the wet. It wasn't Alain's fault but he felt bad, and Pironi never drove again. Prost said it could happen to anybody. Then there was the race in Adelaide where Alain refused to start, and Ayrton hit Brundle – but on the side of Brundle's car, so he lost a wheel. If he'd hit full, then maybe he would have lost his legs. Who knows?'

Ross Brawn has already discussed this feel, although in a more general way. 'We do a lot of reaction training for the starts and Michael's reaction to a light going off is not particularly special. Obviously his reactions to the feel of the car are incredible. It's a feel for what all four tyres are doing and when they've reached the limit of the car. It shows in the fact that he is very quick on the first lap out of the pits. All the other drivers take four or five laps. That's where his talent is most obvious.'

Both Senna and Schumacher had innate skill in the wet from near the beginning of their careers. Senna, competing in a Formula Ford 1600 race at Thruxton, was so fast that Dennis Rushen, co-owner of a Formula 2000 team, went immediately to him afterwards and offered him a drive for the following season at a reduced rate.

Schumacher, competing in a German Formula Ford race at Salzburg, was so fast that Josef Kaufmann, owner of a Formula 3 team, went immediately to him afterwards and offered him a drive for the following season. Kaufmann remembers 'he ran sixth or seventh and worked his way up. To be able to do that is not normal with only a little Formula Ford experience. He'd only done a few races.'

This *feel* seems inborn, not learnt, and if you have it you always have it – if you don't, you never will. Pat Symonds reflects on Schumacher's victory in Spain in the Ferrari in 1996 when, starting third, he almost stalled. From there he rode the storm – visibility in the spray was so bad that he was unaware of how many cars he'd overtaken on the opening lap – and won by 45 seconds.

'You take it as read that he has an incredible natural ability to drive the car. That, to me, is plainly obvious. I think there are other people who have similar abilities to drive a car fast – you can even argue that some may have greater abilities, but they didn't have the complete package. Some of the things that Nigel [Mansell] could do with a car were astounding. Arguably some of them were better than anything Michael's done – but Michael doesn't need to do those things. . . .'

NOTE [1] *The German Grand Prix*, Cyril Posthumus (Temple Press Books, 1966).

Chapter Ten

LESSONS OF HISTORY

'I always relate it to a Sunday afternoon just before 2pm and the race,' Gary Anderson says. 'Take all the Formula 1 drivers, line them up and ask them why they're there. Most of them will look at you gormlessly because they don't *really* know – but Michael does, and even when he was first in the racing car he knew what he was doing, no doubt of that. It's all about getting your head straight and making sure you know. Michael has his head straight. Come 2 o'clock on the Sunday afternoon Michael isn't yapping and shouting and mooching around, he's enjoying himself at being serious.

'People criticise him for his dedication and commitment and all sorts of stuff but they're just jealous, really, because they can't see how important it is. His whole fitness is incredible, for instance. I have seen him in Brazil at six o'clock on a Sunday morning: we're leaving for the track and he's coming back from a run. How many drivers are up at 6am on a Sunday, never mind having a run to loosen themselves up a bit?'

These are formidable words portraying, as they do, a formidable man.

Stirling Moss approaches it from a different direction. 'Jimmy was a racer. One doesn't think of him particularly as a racer but he was. The whole of my career, which was 529 races, I drove against a lot of names, against a lot of fantastic drivers, but only about three or four *racers*.' The words tumble from Moss, precise, urgent. Yes, he will say, Fangio, was a racer too.[1]

So *what is it that makes the racer as against the very good driver?*

Indianapolis 2000, and the United States rediscovers Formula 1 just as Formula 1 rediscovers the United States. Coulthard (left) is about to seize the lead from Schumacher – but he won't be able to keep it.

'Character. What makes one man brave and another man a coward? Why are certain people born with certain attitudes and attributes? My wife is so honest that if I left a diary on the table she wouldn't read it. I would. What makes that difference? Genes, I suppose. I know a guy who ran some stores in the Bahamas and who drove in the speed weekend there[2]. If he had turned his mind to it he could have been a bloody good racer, and I could tell that, not by seeing how he drove but by knowing the person. You see the same in business. There are people who become leaders because that's the way they are. With racers it's no different.

'Graham Hill was exceptionally good: he did more with less talent than any person I can think of, but Graham was not a racer. Graham was an exceptionally good driver in the way that Prost was one of the great drivers, Jackie Stewart another. I don't think these guys were racers. They were fantastic drivers but you have to realise there is a difference. Racers are guys who go out there and bloody well race. "Boy, I'm not going to let you win." That is a mentality: your car might be incapable of winning but you never think in those terms. Schumacher is the same, Ayrton was the same.'

Schumacher starts sixteenth on the grid at Spa. He does not say to himself 'I might as well go home.' He thinks 'how long will it take me to get into the lead?'

'That is the sign of a great racer. He is a person who has sufficient of that to bring him up to the top. Fangio to me was the most difficult one of all, even more difficult than Jimmy, to quantify. With Fangio it may have been that I couldn't speak to him in his own language.[3] Another thing about the great ones: their career graphs go up at a constant rate from the beginning and go up quickly. There are no plateaux as you get with other drivers. They are always going up.'

Moss has neatly separated those he rates the sloggers (Hill) and the technicians (Stewart, Prost) from those few who have quite different basic instincts and obey the phrase *motor race* in its literal sense, everything subordinated to that.[4]

Schumacher's got a wife and two kids, more money than you can shake a stick at, but if you put him into a pressure point he doesn't back off. If it's you and he going towards La Source hairpin . . . .

'. . .I know I'm going to beat him out of it. . . .'
. . .he's not going to back off.

'That's when it's interesting, that's when you come to the situation where you say "I don't bloody well care whether you're Schumacher or not, sod you. No way will you come out first."'

But he's looking across at you saying 'Stirling Moss, sod YOU.'

'No, no, he'll know by the time we go into the corner that I'm going to come out first.'

How?

'Because . . . because it's my business to make him know.'

What if he thinks it's his business to make you know?

'I'll prove him wrong.'

And that's the mind of the racer?

'Yeah. The great thing about racing is the human person. You can test how strong a piece of metal is, you know when it's going to break, but you don't with the human mind. If your life depended on holding onto a bar, how long could you hold it? Now how long could you hold it because your wife is at risk? You can't quantify people. If motor racing is your choice, and you are an extraordinary person, you'll find ways of turning the wick up a bit because it's necessary. That happens.

'I knew there were times when I drove much faster than I'd normally drive. You get to the end of the race and think "Christ, that *was* quick. How did I get there?" You go round a corner, it's just absolutely right and you carry that thing through. You get this rhythm going and it's a rhythm that you don't necessarily have when you're driving fast. If you're lucky – which usually doesn't happen – you click in and you find that it flows, and suddenly the things that were doubtful before are just natural now.

'That is personality, because the difference in speed between Michael Schumacher and even a moderately good driver is not that much – but it is enormous when you try and make it up. That's the point. A tenth of a second isn't

Juan-Manuel Fangio and Stirling Moss (top left) are interviewed by actor James Garner at Long Beach in 1976. All discussions about greatness have to begin with Fangio and Moss. All discussions about greatness have to move on to Jim Clark, here (above right) in France in 1967 with Keith Duckworth (of Cosworth fame) and Graham Hill. Clark seemed to be able to make the Lotus caress a circuit so lightly (above) that, for example, his tyre wear was minimal, and exactly the same on all four tyres. Even tyre technicians found this difficult to believe.

long but you try to gain a tenth of a second. It's enormous. And it gets more enormous when you are of his stature because he's *always* there, always right on it.'

Jackie Stewart is on this same theme. 'Senna very seldom seemed to drive within the car. If you want to look back, and I certainly have, at all the footage of Senna's laps versus Prost's laps when they had on-board cameras, Prost's movement of the steering wheel was at least 50% less than Senna's. Senna was bullying the car everywhere whereas Prost was coaxing it.'

But you were a coaxer.

'Which I think is the best. Jim Clark was a coaxer. Let's talk about the guys with the real heads: Lauda was a clinical thinker, Prost was The Professor, I was a little bit the same way – clinical and analytical about what I did. Jim drove Colin Chapman's cars because he trusted Colin.'

But Clark comes to us as a man who was so naturally gifted that he didn't have to think about it.

'He didn't, but having said that, how do you account for the number of victories he had? I know he drove the best car at the best time, but most of us [the great ones] did. Jimmy had a wonderful car because Chapman was such an extraordinary person. Jim knew how fast to drive – and how slow to drive.'

Schumacher is a coaxer.

'Not like Clark, Prost or even myself. When Schumacher sets his car up I would say the brain of his car is over the front wheels. You see him going into a corner: he turns in very late and very sharp. Now that's partly to do with today's technology but, even so, the brain would be much further forward in his car than it would be in Häkkinen's or Coulthard's – I don't know about Montoya yet.'

In Schumacher's hot qualifying laps you don't feel subtlety.

'But you didn't feel it with Senna either. Senna didn't have the same subtlety as Prost.' Stewart adds: 'All of them have got big minds.'

Moss, incidentally, says that Senna was the greatest racer he saw. I put that to Jo Ramirez who worked with Senna for

Old masters . . . Fangio in 1976 (left) driving the Mercedes W196 from the mid-1950s. Moss in 1977 driving the Maserati 250F, also from the 1950s.

the six seasons Senna was at McLaren. 'I think so, yes. Ayrton hated to be second. That's what eventually took his life – because he *had* to stay in front.'

Moss is not suggesting that he would have run Schumacher off the track to win *La Source*, of course, and for two reasons. Drivers in the 1950s and 1960s wouldn't have survived long in the cars of that time if they did, and people didn't behave like that anyway. 'Consider that Senna and Prost, two of the greatest drivers who have ever lived, both drove each other off the road – or tried to – at 170 miles an hour. I am convinced that if they had driven in my era they wouldn't have done it. It's not just that they'd probably have got killed, it's that it just wasn't the done thing. I think if Schumacher had raced with us he would have driven with the ethics of people of our era.'

Modern safety, and perhaps modern competitiveness, have led Schumacher to do alarming things to protect his lead from the start to the equivalent of *La Source* everywhere, once moving so far over on brother Ralf that closing your eyes was a good idea. I watch film of old races, black and white newsreel stuff, and the rush from the start line is always a flurry of cars travelling in straight lines, looking for advantage but never weaving for position. Then, with a certain decorum, they filter into the first corner one at a time, single file.

In that sense, Schumacher is the opposite. Winning is all, the ethics of sport lost somewhere back there before the mega money, the hype, the television and the PR industry got hold of it and twisted it into, frequently, an ugly thing. Before, in fact, Formula 1 became a cash dispenser. I put it to Moss that we don't really have ethics in the traditional sense at all and he replied 'no, we don't'. Of course Fangio and Moss and Clark wanted to win, but not to the degree of, say, Senna who, after he crashed at Monaco in 1988, was still crying in his apartment when Ramirez rang him *that night*.

'The attitude that Ayrton had, that will to win, he had in go-karts when he was a kid in Brazil, and it lasted all the way to Tamburello,' Ramirez says. 'Schumacher would have had the same when he was in karts. Damon Hill had to really work at this, it didn't come easy to Damon. Alain Prost was so smooth that we used to say to him "tell us when you're doing your quick lap so we'll know which one it is!" Prost had a very different style, not only in the car but out of it. He was very quiet. Ayrton had this will. . . .'

Few doubt that Schumacher has it too, and when he ran into the back of David Coulthard at Spa in the wet in 1998 he detonated. He stormed down the pit lane to confront Coulthard with a wild look about him and had to be restrained. Impossible to imagine Fangio, Moss or Clark doing that – but not Senna. However, like Senna, Schumacher has mellowed with the years to the point where he can drive a whole season with only occasional outrages and controversies.

Moss echoes Stewart's stricture about asking The Biggest Question. 'I don't think you can compare one man in one era with another. It's difficult enough in athletics – Roger Bannister with a miler now[5] – but at least they are running the same distance with virtually the same equipment. In motor racing the eras are quite different. Those of us who overlapped from one era into another obviously made the change without too much difficulty – it was a seamless change – but to take Fangio, Nuvolari or whoever and try them in a modern car isn't feasible. However I believe that if Fangio had raced now he'd have been the same as he was then.'

That's why, with all respect to Moss, I'm pursuing The Question and Schumacher's place in it. You might think, too, that The Five would have shared characteristics.

'That's the most difficult thing I find: not if you look at them physically, not if you look at the way they talk and so on, but inside there must be a common denominator,' Moss says. 'What makes a man a racer – which is what we're talking about – isn't really connected to speed as much as it is to personality. The difference in going round a corner between any of those would be absolutely minimal. In fact it's usually minimal in the top three in any era, but when the chips are down – and you start to talk about a race, passing back markers, when you're going to do *this*, when you're going to do *that* – all those things fall in place. They make him the racer. When I go into a corner with another guy I don't have a doubt, there can't be a doubt, you have to have complete faith. If you are in any doubt you're not a racer.

'The other interesting thing is that you don't find in those people any big-headedness about it. Today the moderate drivers have to convince themselves that they are as good as they think they are. Schumacher doesn't, of course he doesn't. He is that good, and that's the point. It's confidence, not being big-headed.'

Fangio and Moss were gentlemen, Clark was almost painfully shy, Senna understood (and talked of) humility, and Schumacher seems to have his head straight. Have you ever heard any of them boasting?

You might imagine that self-doubt would be completely absent but Stewart does not agree. 'Jim Clark had a lot of self-doubt. I did too. I always thought people were better than I was and it was a question of me having to try harder. Out of a racing car Jimmy couldn't make a decision to save himself. When it was about a girlfriend, when it was about where to go for dinner, when it was about whether to go to a movie, he would not be able to decide.'

I remember you said you were right in the middle of Florida somewhere, Clark driving, and you stopped at a railway line, nothing for a thousand miles each way, and he said 'do you think we should go across?'

'He said "what do you think?" It was single track too! But when he got into a car he drove it with natural skill and mind-management. I don't think he had self-doubts in a racing car, but everything to deal with before getting into the car he had.'

Jo Ramirez gives an anecdote about how ordinary Clark was outside a racing car. 'I first came over [from Mexico] in 1962. I planned to drive but that didn't happen, although I got involved in Grand Prix racing. I became the go-for at Ferrari. There was no way they were going to give me a proper job because I was not Italian and I didn't speak Italian and I had no qualifications! We'd go to the races on the Continent by boat across the Channel. Clark would be on it. We'd sit in the bar and play cards quite normally, because that's the way it was.'

Before we look at specific qualities, Moss explains why

we are talking about so few drivers. 'If you take the greatest singers in the world you've only got three or four, if you take the greatest jugglers in the world you've only got three or four, in every era you never have more than four at most. I think if I'd been more intelligent I could have made a bigger mark – if I'd joined up with factory teams earlier and gone where the main chance was, as Fangio did.'

In that sense, Fangio was very modern indeed.

One common characteristic is that the great drivers have time when they travel at racing speed because to them it is happening slowly. As Jim Endruweit puts it, 'you get the strong impression that Schumacher is driving at, well, nine-tenths.'

I pursued that with Ramirez.

Did you notice that Ayrton had this ability to drive a car 100% but using only 90% of himself, so that he had 10% spare – like Schumacher?

'They do seem to have that.'

It has to mean, and this is where it gets almost scary,

that for most of their career they are driving faster than anybody else but nowhere near their own limit.

'Very true. For example, let me speak about the gismos – active suspension, ride heights and all of that. On the straight Ayrton used to be able to raise the car for maximum speed and lower it for the corner. When he told Gerhard Berger that – because there was a difference in lap times – Gerhard said "bloody hell, you've time to do that?" It was the difference between Ayrton and the rest. Schumacher seems very cool, he doesn't get excited about it. David Coulthard is like that on the radio. Ayrton was excitable, but that was his way.

'You could talk to Ayrton about everything. He was so quick to think and grasp things. Working with him you learned about life.'

Stewart once gave an extraordinary description of how he treated his mind as a balloon and, holding that mental picture, deliberately deflated it. I wondered if he – and Schumacher – can think slowly?

'Yes, of course. God had given me a talent which would allow things to be viewed slowly. Speed didn't exist. A lot of people are not synchronised. How would you like to be receiving a service from Pete Sampras? It would just be a blur of fluff to me. Take Mohammad Ali. He seldom got hit because he saw the punch coming almost from the ankle to the knee to the weight distribution his opponents made for the arm going back, whereas for me it would have been a blur again, and then hospital. But when I was driving a racing car I had all the time in the world to see everything that was required, not just to come off the gas pedal – although coming off the gas pedal was in itself an art whilst not disturbing the car's forward motion to a point where the pitch changed. Nobody ever told me anything about that: it was learning from experience.

'What happens in life – I don't care what it is – is that first of all you have to get experience. It doesn't matter how much natural talent you've got. From experience you gain some knowledge. When you have experience and knowledge you can sometimes accomplish things.

'People talk about reactions but it's somewhat overstated to say *you've got such fast reactions*. It's got nothing to do with the muscular response to any particular situation, it is the consumption of information which that person is getting from his eyes or ears or hands or whatever.'

A television programme in 2001 showed drivers' reactions tested: a piece of paper was dropped without warning and they had to catch it by clapping their hands. Schumacher was no quicker at this than the others.

Clark, Hill and Co. could wander about – but the world was changed by the '90s. Schumacher had to guard the privacy of his family hard, although Corinna smiled for the photographers, and dad Rolf was occasionally caught on camera too. (Below) Still some little way to go. Canada, 1997.

'Right, correct, and that's what I'm saying, but now consider what would happen if you put a few other elements into it. Suppose Schumacher had had to chew gum and walk at the same time as catching the paper. You would have seen him take the lead comfortably. That would be the difference.'

I put it to Ramirez that, without being provocative, Prost didn't have what Senna had in the same way that Häkkinen hasn't got what Schumacher has – a merciless hardness of purpose.

'I think,' Ramirez replied after a long pause for thought, 'one of the things Ayrton had and Schumacher has is this racecraft. They were so much cleverer in being able to pace their own race. You watch Schumacher do a pit stop: he comes in at the last moment, comes quick, gets out quick, doesn't lose any time at all. I remember the Hungarian Grand Prix and it was just unbelievable. They told him on the radio 'you can win if you stop three times – so you can have the car light – but you have to do 19 qualifying laps. And he did it. *Nineteen laps at qualifying speed.* Only once did he have the car sideways, and he never lost it. Ayrton could have done those laps.'

The great ones have 10% left for when they need it.
'They can just turn this on like a tap.'
How? What is that?
'They have their own special limits. For example, Mika hasn't got this racecraft that Schumacher has. Mika needs to

have the character to keep pushing all the time. We had Michael Andretti and when he went away Mika came in at Estoril for the Portuguese Grand Prix [in 1993]. Ayrton had let his guard down, thought this young guy was no competition and Mika outqualified him. I remember at the drivers' meeting Mika had a smile from ear to ear and Gerhard said "I bet you that as long as you live you will never ever beat him again." We went to the Japanese Grand Prix after Portugal and Alain was on pole, Senna second and Mika third. In the race Mika was so far behind Ayrton at the end that it meant he was almost a second a lap slower. Mika knew he'd had absolutely no problem with the car, it was fantastic, but he could not reproduce his qualifying for lap after lap in the race.'

Stewart insists that the leaders in each generation have 'not only been given a natural gift from God – it is certainly not their own doing – but as they sharpen their skills they have also recognised that the single most important thing of all is man management, of how to manicure and massage the talent to a higher level. Now take somebody of immense talent, for example Chris Amon.[6] He had as much if not more skill than many of the top Grand Prix drivers of that day, but he chose the wrong cars with the wrong people. Schumacher wouldn't have done that: he'd only drive for the best. I wouldn't have done it either.

'Some people are natural ball-catchers. Some people are natural golfers or tennis players. They have got what it takes to do that. There is no doubt that Tiger Woods has a particular talent, and Nick Faldo had it, so did Palmer and Nicklaus. In the same way Picasso wasn't a manufactured artist. Neither was Matisse. These are people who have *it*. What did Laurence Olivier have? Something more than everybody else. You could say Gene Kelly had more mind-management than natural talent whereas Fred Astaire had the most wonderful fluidity about his dancing, and that was because he was just so naturally gifted.'

One of the central aspects is whether driving a Grand Prix car is more difficult now than then, something about which Lauda has no doubt. He drove a modern car not so long ago and found the traction control and paddle gearchanging made life much easier.

Nigel Stepney echoes that. At the end of the 2001 season, as we have seen, Schumacher had 43 pole positions compared to Senna's all-time record of 65. 'No,' Stepney said, 'Ayrton's poles total won't be safe. No, nothing's safe. We've got about another three years of Michael to break the poles and he's not that far behind. In three years he can destroy all that if we can do a good enough job and he can keep his act together. I don't see why he shouldn't. However, I still think he's got some things to do which Ayrton just did. I still think Ayrton was the best. Yeah.'

Stepney accepts that they drove in different eras. 'But comparing the two, you have to consider how much help Michael gets with the technology. There was technology years ago, when Ayrton drove, but I'm talking about the *amount*. Michael is not as *manual* as Ayrton: Ayrton did a lot of these things automatically, as did Prost and Lauda and so on, and that is why I still put him that step ahead at the moment. I'm a bit old fashioned about this.'

The great ones have always been alone in what they could do and how they could do it. Schumacher in Malaysia, 2000.

Stewart, ruminating: 'If you have a racing team, and you're spending all that money on technology – more expensive than ever in the history of motorsport – you'd want the best driver even if you had the very best equipment. The reason is that sometimes a less than great driver can win in the very best car, and it happens – the high technology, traction control, ground effects, everything – but if you look back at the people I'm talking about here, they were never multi-World Champions. They were good enough to win a World Championship if they were in a very good car and a very good team. If somebody's got a very good car they show quite well but you haven't seen them win oodles and oodles of Grands Prix, and you haven't seen them win when everything's gone against them. The difference, I think, is that the great drivers have the capacity to move on from their first championship. It takes an immense amount of commitment, it takes an immense amount of determination, single-mindedness. It's sacrificing all sorts of other things.

'At the end of the day there's only six really good drivers on the grid, and out of those six there's maybe only three who are extraordinary but there's always only one genius. Now Schumacher is that genius. I think Häkkinen and Coulthard are the other two in the extraordinary category, while Montoya is up there and Ralf Schumacher is close to being up there.'

The technology became a substitute for skill, and that's why Senna objected to it.

'Yes,' Stewart says, 'but you've still got to look for the fine limit.'

Which explains why, from this theoretical equality, Schumacher has emerged absolutely dominant. He found the fine limit and never forgot where it was.

'He is still able to cream the last little bit out of the milk bar, to take that little bit more out of it than anybody else. What you've got to see is where the cream is lying. Is it in a wee crevasse, is it tucked away where nobody else has noticed it? Will it give me an advantage, be helpful to me? I'll go and look for it and find out where it is and then use the car to take that advantage, which is well hidden from the others. The others are like paper hangers in a thunderstorm [condemned to get wet whatever they do]. They are too busy trying to keep the car on the road to think creatively about where to find an advantage. So it doesn't matter what technology exists: the drivers who are really the best will always take it that little bit further. They won't be flying off the road every five minutes, they won't be one-lap wonders and they won't be one-championship wonders either.'

The matter of difficulty in the cars, then and now, is fascinating.

'Physically you've got power steering, you've got lighter brake pedals, you've got more downforce, more grip, you've got traction control. [At this point in the interview Stewart examined his palms.] 'Still marks there – they bled every race at Monaco and quite a few other racetracks [from gripping the gear knob]. These are just mild differences, however, because we're on a progressive journey from Caracciola[7] and Nuvolari to Fangio and Ascari, then on to Moss and Clark, to Stewart and Fittipaldi, to Prost and Senna. They all had considerably better working environments than the generation before. I had a much

cushier job than Caracciola or Nuvolari, I suspect. That's part of evolution, of the adjustment. In order to get the ultimate in performance, man has always – *always* – surpassed whatever technology has been provided. How do you account for the fact that the 4-minute mile is now a slow mile? Man has always extended beyond, and you can't say it is only the latest running shoe. But in motor racing we've now got telemetry, which is objective measurement.'

Does that make Schumacher better than you?

'It doesn't, but it provides the opportunity of using those mechanical devices more productively.'

You or Clark going round Spa had more freedom of choice about what you'd try to make the car do. Now the car is programmed.

The ten years of Schumacher in Grand Prix racing. The newcomer, 1991. The man with the big future, 1992. The front-runner, 1993. Dressing for a World Championship, 1994 . . .

'You can still lock up your wheel going in to *Pouhon*, or anywhere else for that matter. Whatever the engineers and the R & D department do, the human remains an amazing animal of chameleon skills. These skills adapt to all the idiosyncrasies which the technologists produce, and they have always adapted. These days they are doing it in extremes which are all different.'

Consider the vintage Ferrari in which Schumacher gave a demonstration run at Silverstone in 2001. In 1951 when it raced and won, it covered 90 laps (418km/260m) at an average speed of 154kmh/96mph. The track measured 4.6km/2.8m and pole was 1:43.400s, an average speed of 161kmh/100mph. Silverstone had no chicanes to slow the cars then and comprised straights linked by five corners and two curves, Chapel and Abbey.

At the 2001 Grand Prix, the current Ferrari which Schumacher drove covered 60 laps (308kmh/191m) at an average speed of 214kmh/133mph. The track measured 5.1km/3.2m and pole was 1:20.447s, an average speed of 230kmh/142mph. Silverstone had a whole array of features to slow the cars, including a tight horseshoe at Club, a 90 degree left at Abbey and the contorting Bridge-Luffield complex.

In spite of that, Schumacher got round it more than

40mph faster than the car had done in 1951. These are the extremes which are all different but, as Stewart says, they didn't come from nowhere, they evolved.

To which Stirling Moss says: 'The point is, one learns the tools of one's trade. If you have to cook with a blunt knife, you find different ways of making it cut. It is exactly the same with racing. The technology is a disadvantage for demonstrating a driver's ability: I think that Michael has a greater difficulty now in demonstrating his superiority as blatantly as others in other eras could do. When you start bringing in driver aids, it isn't that the drivers haven't the ability, it's that the best drivers' ability is reduced – or you might say that the lesser drivers' ability is brought up to the common denominator. It negates skill and, expanding on that, I think you'll find that Jacques Villeneuve is against making the circuits too safe: the safer you make them, the greater the contempt of danger you have and, therefore, the drivers' ethics are allowed to lapse.

'The eras change and the style of driving changes and that's why the person who drives today is a glorified go-kart driver – although fantastic in what they do. Fangio would have adapted, I am sure we would, I am sure Jimmy would have done. Of course he would. If that's what you have to do, that's what you do. We had to do things in those days – make allowances because the dampers would get worn and they wouldn't work so well. Things like that don't exist today. When disc brakes came in we learned disc brakes – they were much better than others. But it came in small increments.'

Jo Ramirez has seen every Formula 1 car since 1962 and I wondered if he thought that Clark could have driven Häkkinen's 2001 McLaren, and Häkkinen could have driven Clark's mid-1960s Lotus, without too much difficulty?

'There would be more chance that Clark could have driven Mika's car than the other way round. The cars of today are easier to drive: then they were not easy to drive. The balance of the car was much more critical. They were less forgiving, the tyres were not so good – the tyres were narrow! – and you had to change gears like they don't do now. Changing gear was an art. There were people like Clark and Senna who could change in the middle of a corner to maximise the power of the engine – and

everybody says you don't change gear in the corners, you do it before or after. I feel you can learn your trade, and the more you do it the better you get. But at the end of the day nobody is going to teach you how to drive a car better, you have to teach yourself, and from driving it better you can become absolutely superb at it.'

At the Jaguar launch in 2002, Eddie Irvine was questioned about the team principal, Niki Lauda, who intended to drive a modern Formula 1 car hard (he'd done this before, but evidently not *hard*) in order to understand better what the drivers of today were talking about. In the course of his answer Irvine said the cars in Lauda's era were much easier to drive and he knew because he'd driven some. They were like 'saloons'. This runs counter to everything just about anybody has ever said on the subject and,

The ten years of Schumacher in Grand Prix racing. Showing them how it's done, Argentina, 1995. The face has filled out, 1995. The lanky kid is long gone, 1996 . . .

suspecting that Irvine might have said it for just such a reason, I asked him to explain.

'The people who say it was more difficult have probably never done it. The cars were very soft, they weren't as knife-edge to drive, they were very progressive. That's why you could see them going sideways. You watch old film on TV and it's very obvious. They reacted very slowly. Changing gears? You can change gear in your car, can't you? That's the least of your worries. The braking was a lot easier then because they didn't have the stopping power that they have now. You backed off a bit earlier and feathered it through.'

Interesting, as they say.

The modern racing driver, particularly if he achieves the status and global recognition of Schumacher, risks being overwhelmed – mobbed – unless he controls his life very carefully. Essentially this means living in a sort of seclusion. Evidently even Monte Carlo became too much for Schumacher and he has retreated to his home in Switzerland from within which he is able to live a family life.

Ramirez ruminates that the modern successful drivers 'cannot appreciate their own wealth because they've always had it. They say Schumacher was very upset about what happened on 11 September [the terrorist attacks in the United States]. I'm sure he was. Maybe it was because he'd

never experienced the real world, whereas Ayrton had been exposed to it in Brazil even though he came from a wealthy family. In fact Ayrton was more exposed to life and he had to work for it a little harder than Schumacher.'

To which Jackie Stewart adds: 'You could say Schumacher's got all the money he needs, he's got a family, he's got everything else and driving a Grand Prix car is safer than fishing, or rugby, or boxing, or mountaineering.

'Does he want to continue to drive himself and only be interested in a single-minded way? I think he is limited to one area of performance and I don't think he has great ambitions to say "oh, I really would love to do this" about something else. For example he goes up to Norway for the winter and gets away from everybody else, so he doesn't want to go to dinner parties, he doesn't want to go to cocktail parties, he doesn't want to meet anybody else that's famous: no ambitions in that respect. He doesn't want to build a skyscraper. Ayrton was beginning to be quite interested in business, interested in things beyond the pit and paddock.

'I don't think Schumacher's got a lot of curiosity, and that's the thing which attracts most people to look at other things. You're curious. *What does it take to do this*, or *why would you do that?* It's nothing to do with money. When I did that movie with Roman Polanski[8] I thought: Roman Polanski's so clever and such a creator that it would be really nice to work with somebody like him. It gave me another dimension.'

You have mastered the art of public speaking.

'I'm sure Michael isn't interested in doing that, because if he was he'd have done it. If he'd like to speak at the United Nations he could. I spoke to 8,000 people recently and to do that you've got to be pretty sure you've got your priorities together – it's live, it's not recorded. You've got to do it right, and to do that you've got to have a desire to do it. I'm not sure Michael has reached that point – but it may come.

'I'm talking about beyond doing expert commentaries on the races on TV – that would be the easy option, as James Hunt did and Martin Brundle is doing, but Martin does other things, TV programmes which aren't about racing. And he has a business, and he's with the BRDC.[9] That's

because you're curious, you want to try and do other things. I don't think Michael is interested in looking at other people's views in a way that would allow him to be exposed to them, even in a peripheral way. For me, he should be improving himself. You could say that he doesn't need self-improvement but I think everybody needs it.'

He's got his place in Switzerland and he only seems to need to move around within the Grand Prix world or go to far away places to get fit in the winter.

'That's where I think he is missing such a lot, with the entrée that he has. In that sense he could be very big and multi-coloured, a kaleidoscope if he wanted, but at the moment it's very mono-colour. It's bright red. When I met Polanski I was interested in listening to Polanski. When I met the King of Jordan I just wanted to be exposed to the King or Jordan as much as I could. You don't prostitute yourself for that – because he wanted to meet me, in the same way that somebody would want to meet Michael. Having met them you develop within yourself. My hope is that Michael will develop from where he is, because not every sportsman does that. It's a rarity, but it is also important, because when you're a sportsman you're so spoiled.'

The ten years of Schumacher in Grand Prix racing. Easy does it, 1997. The smile, 1999. Question and answer, 2000. The matured man, 2001.

Now, maybe, we can reach towards a conclusion, which of course is not the same thing as the answer to The Biggest Question.

We've examined the cars of different eras, and compared the driving of them. We haven't considered how strong the competition was, and Gary Anderson offers cautionary words about that in a general reflection. 'With a lot of sports you have easier opportunities than motor racing. How many people are out there playing golf at different levels before you get to the top? And think how much cheaper it is to do, because you only need a set of golf clubs. In tennis it's a racket, in soccer a football and so on. You don't need £10,000s in equipment before you can compete – and, incidentally, the more equipment you need, the greater the risk of some of it being bad! The guys who get to the top in motor racing aren't necessarily the good guys. The odd one does – like Michael.'

Even keeping these words in mind, Fangio had to compete against Moss (and vice versa, of course) but also Ascari, the ferocious Giuseppe Farina, Mike Hawthorn and Peter Collins. Clark had Graham Hill, John Surtees, Jack Brabham and Stewart.

Now listen to Jo Ramirez. 'I spoke to Alain before Senna came to McLaren [in 1988] and he said "I'll have anybody". Schumacher won the championship two years against Damon Hill, two years against Mika Häkkinen – well, one year against David Coulthard. I'm not taking anything away from those guys, but I am saying they were the only ones Schumacher had to race against. Senna raced against Prost, against Mansell, against Piquet, against Rosberg, all of those people who were top guys. They were winning Grands Prix and championships.'

Stewart insists that 'there's nobody as close to Schumacher' – in terms of ability – 'as there was to Senna' and Moss reinforces that. 'The thing that Michael has at the moment is the biggest gap between himself and the next guy, the number 2 to him if you like. It may be closing, it may not, but if you go back six months or a year the guy you consider number 2 – Mika or David or whoever – was nowhere near Michael's ability, and that's the gap.'

Jody Scheckter reinforces *that*. 'It could be said that he is the best driver of all times. However, Ayrton Senna was racing against Alain Prost and vice versa, and they could both be contenders for the best. Michael is not up against that level of competition. That is the only argument against him being the best of all time.'

Gary Anderson invokes Prost and Senna, but in a different way. 'I think you have to consider Michael among the greatest drivers since 1950 and I don't think we've seen the end of it yet. I'm putting Michael in front of Ayrton. He's more complete. If you took Senna and Prost – Senna was the ultimate go-out-and-do-the-job, pick it up and throw it round, and Prost was The Professor. Michael is a combination of both of them.'

Jean-Louis Schlesser who was at Mercedes in sports cars at the same time as Schumacher – and nearly got on the wrong end of Derek Warwick's wrath when Schumacher ought to have been the recipient – has been watching motorsport these many years as well as competing. 'If you want to compare Schumacher with somebody, and it's very hard, there is one guy. Fangio. For me he was something absolutely special because he won five titles with different cars. You remember when the Maserati was a piece of rubbish, nobody wanted it, and he made the car into a winner. Jim Clark also was something exceptional. I was very young when I saw him but he impressed me a lot. You can put Schumacher at the top, you can put Schumacher with Fangio.'

The implication is that Schumacher joins Fangio, not supplants him.

Stirling Moss does not agree. 'He is an exceptional driver and in the top six of all time but he has nowhere near the ability of Fangio. In my mind Fangio was the greatest driver. I don't even know if Michael's reached the ability of Senna, I don't know if he's reached the ability of Clark.' Moss says this while accepting that Schumacher could beat Fangio's five championships and Senna's 65 poles.

Stewart agrees. 'There are 17 races a year, 16 minimum. If Ferrari are able to keep the edge, and Schumacher keeps his, it's very possible – because he's being very focused and very aggressive and demanding and unyielding. That's what keeps a team like Ferrari on that edge and that's where it is possible.' This does not lure Stewart into answering The Question, however. Instead he repeats: 'All you can do is give the ones who dominated in their eras. Who were the absolute leaders during that period? Who were the dominant individuals?'

In every sport which can be measured, *everything* has improved to a degree which is almost embarrassing in any comparison between then and now. I've covered Roger Bannister's mile in a footnote so here's another

example, this one chosen at random. In 1928 the great Finnish runner Parvo Nurmi won the 10,000 metre Olympic title with a time of 30m 18.8secs. The current world record, held by Haile Gebrselassie, stands at 26m 22.75secs – nearly four minutes faster. He'd have beaten Nurmi by more than three laps of the track. And so it goes, everywhere you look.

Why should this – mysteriously and suspiciously – not apply to those sports which cannot be measured, the football, the cricket, the tennis and the golf? And where does that leave the racing driver, always a prisoner of the car he has to drive? The world of Nurmi was simplicity itself. He ran. The world of Fangio was complicated by what he could make the car do, and that's the same for Schumacher. In that sense, the faster lap times argue for the impact of technology rather than a parallel increase in driving skill.

I think the crucial difference is that Fangio had scope to be a genius because the circumstances – cars, rules, circuits, attitudes, demands – were looser. Schumacher has conjured beautiful, magical races out of tightness: car construction controlled, a thick book of rules, electronic aids equalising ability, circuits neutered for safety, attitudes born of business, plus voracious demands on every aspect of him every moment.

Perhaps that is a clue.

Fangio was the undisputed master before technology became dominant, Schumacher is the undisputed master after it became dominant, so that, between them, they cover the two most distinctive eras. Moss, Clark and Senna fall quite naturally into the evolution between. If you accept this, you are left with just the two, Fangio and Schumacher. Which?

Nobody knows that.

NOTES

1 Among the few racers he encountered, Moss places Jean Behra, the Frenchman who drove in 52 Grands Prix before being killed at the Avus circuit, Berlin, in 1959.

2 Bahamas Speed Week, in fact known as the Nassau Speed Week. In 1959, en route to the US Grand Prix at Sebring, Florida, Jack Brabham went to it and wrote (in *When the Flag Drops*, William Kimber, 1971) 'I rested on the Saturday in preparation for the International Nassau Trophy, the main event on the Sunday. The race was originally scheduled for 56 laps (250 miles) but eventually it was curtailed to 49 laps and ended at 5.30pm because of bad light. Sixty-five drivers took part: they included Moss.' The cars included Porsches, Aston Martins and Ferraris.

Belgium 2001, proving that the shortest route between two points is over the kerbs. In the race Schumacher stroked the Ferrari home ahead of David Coulthard in the McLaren.

3 Fangio's native language was Spanish and in those days English had not yet become a necessity for anyone within motorsport.

4 In this chapter I have confined myself to drivers of the World Championship, which began in 1950. By definition that excludes all the pre-War drivers, and so we don't have Tazio Nuvolari who was great by any definition. He was a racer and regularly drove cars to destruction rather than finish second.

5 Roger Bannister (now Sir) ran the first 4-minute mile at Oxford in 1954. He did 3m 59.4 and was so exhausted he virtually collapsed. The current record [in January 2002] is held by the Moroccan Hicham El Guerrouj who, at Rome in 1999, did 3m 43.13. The difference in the two times – slightly over 16 seconds – is difficult to even imagine.

6 Chris Amon, a popular New Zealander, drove 96 Grands Prix between 1963 and 1976 – changing teams frequently – but never won a race.

7 Rudi Caracciola (1901–1959) was a highly talented German driver of the 1930s.

8 Roman Polanski, the Polish film director of such films as *Repulsion* (with Catherine Deneuve) and *Rosemary's Baby* (with Mia Farrow) made a documentary about Stewart's weekend at the Monaco Grand Prix in the early 1970s.

9 British Racing Drivers' Club, based at Silverstone.

Facts of the matter

Health warning: statistics can seriously damage your judgement. This part, written before the 2002 season, is not designed to raise the blood pressure.

By coincidence, Senna and Schumacher both competed in 161 Grands Prix, vastly more than Fangio, Moss or Clark – as you can see.

	Races	Poles	Wins	Champs
Fangio	51	29	24	5
Moss	66	16	16	0
Clark	72	33	25	2
Senna	161	65	41	3
Schumacher	161	43	53	4

Statistics *are* potentially dangerous. The table, for instance, might suggest that Moss ought not to be in it at all. Even the most cursory glance, however, shows the extraordinary monument which Fangio built. Projecting from those figures, here might have been the totals if Fangio, Moss and Clark had driven 161 Grands Prix:

	Races	Poles	Wins	Champs
Fangio	161	92	76	9
Moss	161	39	39	0
Clark	161	74	56	3
Senna	161	65	41	3
Schumacher	161	43	53	4

Fangio's total of nine championships is calculated like this. In his career he competed for eight seasons, winning five titles – that's one every 1.6 seasons. It would have taken him some seven further seasons at the modern arrangement of 16 races a season to reach 161 races, and those additional seven seasons yield a figure of 4.3. I have rounded it down to 4.

Clark would have needed a further five and a half seasons to reach the 161 races. His career spanned nine seasons, yielding the two championships. At that average

the extra five and a half would have produced one more.

Now imagine that Senna had been able to continue for three seasons longer than he did, because it's a reasonable assumption he would have done. Schumacher could be looking at:

	Races	Poles	Wins	Champs
Senna	209	84	53	4

Now project Schumacher forward three seasons, because it's a reasonable assumption he will continue that long and, with all the variables, you might have:

	Races	Poles	Wins	Champs
Schumacher	209	55	68	5

These two totals are calculated on the whole of their careers, embracing the start when they weren't winning. That lowers their average and makes projection problematical. Using Schumacher's last three seasons as a more accurate guide, the future might look something like this:

	Races	Poles	Wins	Champs
Schumacher	209	66	72	6

That may be the answer to The Biggest Question, because no such totals have ever been seen before. They will be hard to argue against. We'll have to contain ourselves until the end of 2004 to know, but it will be well worth the wait.

Just to round the subject off, and repeating the health warning that this is all a bit of game-playing which might – inadvertently, almost subconsciously – reveal something important, here are the respective striking rates of wins: Fangio every 2.1 races, Moss every 4.1, Clark every 2.8, Senna every 3.9, Schumacher every 3.0. Compare that with Mika Häkkinen – 20 wins from his 161 races – and it's 8.0. That's the difference.

Rubens Barrichello and Jean Todt help Schumacher celebrate his *fourth World Championship, in Hungary, 2001. Wet faces, big smile.*

STATISTICS

Michael Schumacher's career as at 1 January 2002

Karting

1984 German Junior Champion
1985 German Junior Champion; Junior World Championship, 2nd
1986 German Senior Championship, 3rd; European Championship, 3rd
1987 German Senior Champion and European Champion

The cars

1988 Formula Koenig Champion; European Formula Ford, 2nd
1989 German F3, joint 2nd
1990 German F3 Champion; World Sports Car Championship, joint 5th; International F3, Macau, 1st; International F3, Fuji, 1st
1991 World Sports Car Championship, joint 9th; F1 début, Jordan, Benetton, 5 races. F1 drivers' championship, joint 12th

Grand Prix racing

1992 Benetton, 3rd (win, Belgium)
1993 Benetton, 4th (win, Portugal)
1994 Benetton, 1st (wins, Brazil, Pacific, San Marino, Monaco, Canada, France, Hungary, Belgium*, Europe)
1995 Benetton, 1st (wins, Brazil, Spain, Monaco, France, Germany, Belgium, Europe, Pacific, Japan)
1996 Ferrari, 3rd (wins, Spain, Belgium, Italy)
1997 Ferrari, 2nd ** (wins, Monaco, Canada, France, Belgium, Japan)
1998 Ferrari, 2nd (wins Argentina, Canada, France, Britain, Hungary, Italy)
1999 Ferrari, 5th (wins San Marino, Monaco)
2000 Ferrari, 1st (wins, Australia, Brazil, San Marino, Europe, Canada, Italy, USA, Japan, Malaysia)
2001 see separate panel
* Disqualified
** Excluded from the final classification for crashing into Jacques Villeneuve in Jerez).

The record-breaking year – 2001 Ferrari

4 Mar	Australia, Melbourne	P/FL/1
18 Mar	Malaysia, Sepang	P/1
1 Apr	Brazil, Interlagos	P/2
15 Apr	San Marino, Imola	DNF
29 Apr	Spain, Barcelona	P/FL/1
13 May	Austria, A1-Ring	P/2
27 May	Monaco, Monte Carlo	1
10 June	Canada, Montreal	P/2
24 June	Europe, Nürburgring	P/1
1 July	France, Magny-Cours	1
15 July	Britain, Silverstone	P/2
29 July	German, Hockenheim	DNF
19 Aug	Hungary, Hungaroring	P/1
2 Sept	Belgium, Spa	FL/1
16 Sept	Italy, Monza	4
30 Sept	USA, Indianapolis	P/2
14 Oct	Japan, Suzuka	P/1

Championship: Schumacher 123 points, David Coulthard (McLaren) 65, Rubens Barrichello (Ferrari) 56.

Grand Prix totals

161 races:	(although David Hayhoe gives it as 162 – a fine point, because in 1996 in France the Ferrari expired on the formation lap)
Wins:	53 (world record, beating Alain Prost, 51)
Poles:	43
Fastest laps:	44 (world record, beating Prost, 41)
Points:	801 (world record, beating Prost, 798.5)

They don't say   a pit stop in 1994
how many helpers   on the way
you need to   to winning the
break records.   Pacific Grand Prix
Schumacher makes   at Aida, Japan.

INDEX